SHELL

Shell

One Woman's Final Year After a Lifelong

Struggle With Anorexia and Bulimia

MICHELLE STEWART

Published by LifeTree Media Ltd.
www.lifetreemedia.com

Distributed by Greystone Books Ltd.
www.greystonebooks.com

Cataloguing data available from Library and Archives Canada
ISBN 978-1-928055-13-6 (paperback)
ISBN 978-1-928055-14-3 (epub)
ISBN 978-1-928055-15-0 (PDF)

Editing by Maggie Langrick
Copyediting by Carol Volkart
Cover design by David Drummond
Interior design by Ingrid Paulson
Printed and bound in Canada by Friesens

Contents

JUNE 2013

JULY 2013

AUGUST 2013

SEPTEMBER 2013

OCTOBER 2013

NOVEMBER 2013

FEBRUARY 2014

MARCH 2014

APRIL 2014

EPILOGUE

Foreword

This compelling story of the last year in the life of an individual dying from her chronic anorexia and bulimia is at once spellbinding and terribly sad. While the author does not deliberately dwell on her eating disorder, to me it shouts out from every page as the most consistent aspect of the final part of her life. Michelle Stewart's heartbreaking acknowledgment in an entry when it is clear her renal failure has progressed to the point that she has little time remaining that she continues to weigh herself four times per day and restrict her eating to attempt to avoid gaining weight is a telling commentary on the vicious grip that anorexia exerts on its victims.

Of course this grip is evident in so many ways in Michelle's life. Her decision to not have life-saving dialysis because it would require some changes in her eating is her anorexia in direct action. The disruption of so many relationships, and so many aspects of her life over decades is a direct consequence of her condition. As she attempts to have the best life she can have, her dual eating disorder is her constant companion—her worst best friend ever.

Anorexia nervosa, along with its related diagnoses of bulimia and other forms of eating disorder, is a serious medical illness with significant mortality and endless suffering. The death rate from eating disorders is between 10 and 20 per cent, making it one of the most lethal psychiatric conditions. The rate of development of chronic, intractable illness is an additional 10 to 15 per cent. These latter individuals struggle to uphold their quality of life in the face of seemingly insurmountable obstacles.

The illness has been reported in medical literature since the late 1600s, and occurs all over the world in both men and women. It is recognized wherever there is a segment of society that has adequate access to food, and where starvation is rare. Although the manifestations of this illness are somewhat affected by local cultures, its form is overwhelmingly so similar across regional boundaries that it remains one of the most identifiable psychiatric conditions. When examined genetically, the proportion of risk for eating disorders attributable to underlying genetic vulnerability is 75 to 80 per cent, the highest of any psychiatric illness.

Despite these facts, individuals with anorexia and bulimia face discrimination at multiple levels. The first of those arises when family, society and even the health-care system questions whether the condition is actually an illness at all, mistakenly asserting that it is a voluntary choice on the part of the sufferer. This is a soul-destroying situation for the affected individual, causing her to invalidate her own suffering, and making her reluctant to seek out help.

The author describes clearly the sequence of a sexual assault leading to the development of her fatal eating disorder, and makes it clear throughout the book that the condition is "not really about the food." Rather, food is a symptom of all the other things that were wrong when she fell ill, and which have gone wrong since, none of which ever received adequate attention from her health-care providers, over so many years of treatment.

When a sufferer of eating disorders does come to seek treatment, a second layer of discrimination comes into play. Access to effective treatment is non-existent throughout many parts of Canada, and where treatment exists, there are long waiting periods, even for those most severely affected. Well-meaning but poorly trained individuals who end up attempting to look after these individuals often make damaging suggestions, such as the one made to Michelle Stewart—although she was a survivor of sexual assault—that getting a boyfriend and having sex might help her recover from her illness. Other practitioners will hold on to outdated theories about the cause of anorexia and lay the blame on the victim's family, alienating the patient from his or her most important source of support and assistance through recovery.

And why are practitioners so poorly prepared? In Toronto, which hosts the largest program for anorexia in Canada, medical students receive no education about eating disorders. Family Medicine residents receive no formal education in eating disorders. The psychiatric training program, one of the largest in North America, devotes a total of three hours out of a five-year program to eating disorders education. Most residents graduating from this program have never seen an individual with anorexia.

Finally, there is the systemic discrimination against those with this type of psychiatric disorder, which is especially prevalent in young female sufferers of mental illnesses. If anorexia were an illness primarily affecting middle-aged men—as is prostate cancer, for example—I believe there would be a clinic in every hospital in the country, and riots in the street if there were delays in treatment. The mortality from anorexia is in the same range as that for prostate cancer.

A final source of discrimination, which is particularly shattering for many patients, is the notion that recovery from anorexia is not possible, and that the best a sufferer can hope for is to learn to "live with her illness." Although it is totally untrue, this view is endorsed by well-meaning but poorly informed health-care practitioners who, lacking training and experience, do not see good results in their own practice, and thus assume that a good result is not achievable. This robs the affected person of any hope for the future, and all too many of those who suffer make the choice made by Michelle to "make the best of it," and simply struggle to do the best they can for as long as possible.

Recovery from anorexia is definitely possible—in fact, it is the most common outcome overall. While earlier detection and treatment is associated with a greater likelihood of recovery, I have seen patients who have been ill for more than 40 years make complete recoveries. Most recoveries occur sometime in the first 15 years' duration of illness, and the average time to recover is six to seven years after the onset of the condition. The overall rate of recovery is 60 to 70 per cent. So I rarely advise families or patients to accept their condition as untreatable, especially if they are young.

What does recovery look like? After one year, the patient will talk about the challenges of maintaining a recovered state, and although she or he has some confidence that it can be maintained, there may still be a feeling of hesitancy. She may have occasional bad days, and some ongoing concerns about her body, but she is aware that her life is moving forward in a positive way.

After two years, most recovered individuals will tell me that they feel very solid in their recovery and comfortable in their body, and that they really no longer think about food, weight or shape. They tell me a lot about their "new" life.

After five years, most recovered individuals tell me that they can barely remember having been ill; that it seems like a dream, like it happened to someone else. They tend to tell me a lot about how their life has been going since they got better. This is the state that individuals suffering from this terrible illness can and should hope for.

Families usually play a critical role in recovery, even of adult patients. While some families are suffering under the burdens of other illnesses, divorce or separation, and may include actively abusive individuals, the overwhelming majority of families are well-meaning and loving, and will do anything to help affected individuals. Unfortunately, some actions that might come naturally are all too often exactly the wrong thing to do. For example, locking the fridge to prevent binge eating is usually a mistake, as is attempting to view dietary restriction as "bad" behaviour and trying to punish it away. To truly support the sick person, families need and deserve help and accurate information, not only about the nature of the illness, but also about how they can help. I have met so many families over the years who have resolutely hung on, doing everything they could for their affected child, for years and even decades . . . never losing hope, and never, ever giving up.

New-onset anorexia is rare past the age of 40. However, the rate of development of chronic illness due to anorexia and bulimia later in life is high, perhaps in the 20-to-30-per-cent range. While some victims of anorexia and bulimia will die at younger ages, many do continue on into middle life very ill, as Michelle did.

The incidence of anorexia increased sharply in the 1970s and 1980s. The first wave of that cohort is now in middle life, and a proportion of them are seeking medical help for their disorders now for the first time, with long-standing established illness. As Michelle so eloquently describes, access to high-quality diagnosis and treatment was rare in the early years of her illness, when she had the best chance of a recovery. Many of those affected are never diagnosed at a younger age, and only present when some major medical problem arises in their late 30s or early 40s, and the diagnosis is finally made.

Do I disagree with the author's decision to avoid treatment that might have saved—or at least prolonged—her life? Not necessarily. Having worked in the field of eating disorders for nearly 30 years, I have had the privilege of knowing many individuals with anorexia nervosa, many of whom have suffered for decades.

I urge any individual with anorexia not to give up hope of recovery, especially when no permanent damage to the body has yet been done. And while I am ever hopeful, even for individuals who have been ill for many, many years, for some, a time comes where further efforts at treatment seem futile, or when, as in Michelle's case, some permanent and irreversible damage occurs that is not compatible with a meaningful extension of life. These are difficult situations. At some point in the late 30s, if it appears that their life is in danger, I will have a discussion with my patients about how they wish to proceed. Many patients immediately identify that they want interventions. Some are in denial that anything could go wrong. Others have more ambivalence, and the discussion goes on for some time. For a few, the immediate answer is to not intervene, and let the illness take its course. In my experience, few will identify that they are dying, until there is irrefutable proof for that to be the case. Michelle falls into the latter category. So I would view her decision as rational, and if she had been under my care I would not have protested . . . but would have indicated that she could change her mind at any time to choose instead to actively pursue a life-prolonging course of treatment.

So was her decision courageous? Perhaps realistic is a better word. She seems to have examined her options, after 30 years of illness, and decided that the likelihood of a meaningful extension of life, with a reasonable quality of life, was low. This is a decision made by many, and her account resonates with all that such a decision to forgo ongoing medical treatment entails.

I think it is important for those reading this volume to understand that death is not the only outcome in anorexia, nor chronic illness. There is hope for a life free of illness, a life that is happy and fulfilling, without the burden of this terrible disease. And that even after long periods of illness, that hope still exists for so many sufferers.

And still . . . I find it difficult to put aside the entry, where faced with so little time remaining, she compellingly describes the extent to which her anorexia so completely fills her life and her thoughts. It is everywhere, and is more important than anything. It doesn't matter that she is at her lowest adult weight—far below the imaginary target her illness set for her—nor that she has an intellectual understanding about what is happening to her body. Her anorexia continues to torment her, and tell her she is bad, and a failure. And in this way, she is denied some of the peace and acceptance that should be a part of her year's journey.

D. Blake Woodside MD FRCPC
Medical Director Emeritus, Program for Eating Disorders,
Toronto General Hospital
Professor, Department of Psychiatry,
University of Toronto

April 2015

Prologue

Take a certain set of genetics, combine it with the right triggers and a dose of family dynamics, add unattainable societal standards of beauty and the culture of "thin is in," and you have a recipe for an eating disorder.

How do *you* see anorexia? Would you consider it a lifestyle? The result of wilful bad choices? An avoidable condition that with a bit of pull-yourself-up-by-your-bootstraps tenacity could be snapped into submission? A disease? Believe me, nobody thinks that last one.

In all my years working inside the health-care system, I learned that every illness, every organ, has a pecking order. This is not a judgment, just a fact. Look at where the majority of research dollars go and how the health-care budget is divided. Cancer has more cache than syphilis.

I am not pooh-poohing cancer research, simply saying that we prioritize our expenditures in the way we do because there is always a judgment involved. How does throwing money at people who you might rightly predict have a strong probability of relapse compare to a "clean" investment in a targeted screening program through which you could measurably improve survival rates for, say, prostate cancer? Faced with the question of which program to back, which would you choose?

We are comfortable with the illnesses that we can manipulate with drugs, devices and procedures in which parts are taken out or new parts put in. We are less enthusiastic in dealing with the big black hole that things like eating disorders represent. Nor, I suspect, do people fully appreciate the magnitude of the toll they take on the body and its associated costs; a toll which obviously grows more significant the longer they drag on.

In the early stages of my eating disorder, I must admit I was not focused on its health consequences. But after dipping my toe in the treatment pool and exposing myself to other patients, it didn't take long before I was sure it would kill me, a feeling that would become increasingly deeply buried over time.

I also didn't expect for a moment that I might continue to function—albeit not optimally, of course—for 32 more years before the full consequences would reveal themselves. I never imagined that I might live out a life that was constantly clouded by the image I had in my mind of what I would have been, the risks I would have taken, the mistakes I wouldn't have made, the professional mountains I would have conquered, and the relationships I would have embraced more fully had I been well. In so many ways it has felt as though when I was 16 the life that I should have led died, while my body somehow soldiered on. I have had a 32-year dress rehearsal for the fate I now face.

I recently happened upon an article from a national eating disorder organization website in the U.S. offering guidelines for sufferers on how to tell their story responsibly. It had some advice around avoiding triggering language, etc., which was all very practical. The underlying message is that one must not share information in a manner that might rob other sufferers of hope.

In the blog universe, one doesn't think a lot about the "rules," even though I try to be mindful of my effect on others. I wouldn't want to inadvertently suggest that because my story may not have the happiest of endings, others should aspire to this same fate or determine all hope is lost. Despite the prevalence of these conditions, many people have recovered, and will recover, from eating disorders and will find a way to rebuild their lives without this heavy burden. Through the strength of their own will, with the right supports at the right time, they can and do prevail.

My story is just that: a collection of thoughts and musings that reflect only my experience—it is not intended to serve as a proxy for an entire community of people who share elements of the battles I failed to conquer.

For me, it is more important to say that this is not the sum of my life or who I am. For me it was the hiding, the shame, the debilitating toll of my secrets that in some respects took a greater toll on me than the illness itself. They kept me separated from many people and experiences that are only resurfacing at this time.

Yes, I am a reminder of the physical consequences of this condition—that a reckoning can and will come. And yet even with all of it—the shock, the pain and the sorrow—there is an opportunity for something greater, something deeper that I am still discovering. I am coming to terms with what and who is valuable in my life; with what needs to be saved and what I can let go of. I am learning that little dreams are just as real as big ones. That there is freedom in thinking just about the present moment, without the burden of constantly fast-forwarding into a future that has its own designs. I am seeing perfectionism for the tyranny that it is.

Whether or not I followed the "rules," I need to tell my story my way . . . until the story ends.

If this is the beginning of the end
Then let me write this down
And leave behind
Some sign of an explanation
As to why I would have deliberately
Set my life on this course
I willingly took these actions
I have no other blame than my heart
My mind surely knows better
I can't begin to tell you
What fuels these engines
That roar into life
With every dangerous temptation
How standing on a ledge
Provides me with a view
That I have to see
To feel alive

May
2013

When You're Dying and You Know It…

Clapping hands just somehow doesn't seem appropriate.

It has been about six weeks since my world started turning in a different direction with the news that I have end-stage renal disease.

I am still processing what this means, at times numb, resigned, overwhelmed and horribly sad. Even my moments of happiness are tinged with the stain of a gnawing awareness that my life is coming to an end. I struggle to find meaning in any of it, meaning that just won't come.

Of course, we know we are all mortal and that this ride doesn't last forever. But let me just say it becomes a new shade of real when a doctor sits at his desk and reminds you that you haven't asked him how long you have. (His answer: months, a year…he cannot say.)

Of course there are options—not a cure, mind you, but options: dialysis, transplants. One could give one's body over to a desperate and expensive bid to hang on for a few more months, maybe even years, fighting the infections, dealing with the side-effects of the drugs, until the moment when they just don't work anymore.

Late one night while I was in the hospital, a nurse who knew I was struggling with an IV asked me gently whether I knew I could say "no." The concept was revelatory. I could choose. I had power in a powerless situation. So I told them to take it out, and I understood in that moment no matter what comes next, nothing will happen unless I choose it. For now, I choose to be here. And that is enough.

. . . .

WEDNESDAY, MAY 15
The Care in Health Care

I have two of the world's greatest doctors. My family doctor, on learning my news, sat with me in her office and cried along with me. I suspect, sadly, that is not a typical response. She cares for me in ways that are about so much more than body parts and test results, and her connection to me is one of the things I treasure most. So on the morning I learned my kidneys were failing and found myself an hour later admitted to hospital and waiting to meet the specialist, I was more than a little fearful about who I would find.

Fortunately, it was love at first sight. Not only is he considered the best in his field, but he is warm and funny, and does not shy away from telling me directly what I need to hear, whether I like it or not.

Although he admits he struggles with my stance of seeking only "conservative measures" (code for "no intervention"), looking at my GFR numbers—the numbers that estimate current kidney function—he told me yesterday that he's had patients with numbers as low as mine who have carried on for five or six years. We both know that may not be my story, but for today it gives me a little ray of light where there was none.

I don't know what fate brought these two people into my life, but for today let me say I could not be more grateful.

Desperately Seeking Skinny

They say the truth shall set you free, so now, borrowing from Stephen Colbert, here is a touch of "truthiness."

Few of the people who are aware of my failing kidneys can understand how this could have happened. How does one suddenly discover, seemingly out of the blue, that vital organs are shutting down?

The truth is that this condition is the result of a 32-year unrelenting and painful quest to be thin. Anorexic, bulimic... name a label. I've had them all. These are words that represent to me profound shame and, worse, a lifetime of lost energy and opportunity that can never be reclaimed.

In an ironic twist, "managing" issues related to adults with chronic eating disorders was one of my responsibilities as communications director with the British Columbia Ministry of Health. I would staunchly defend what little is offered to support those struggling individuals, never letting on that I was one myself.

In the early stages of my eating disorder, long ago at age 16, I was referred to the leading "expert" at BC Children's Hospital, who suggested that if I had sex it would get better. (He was later driven out of the profession.)

This began a cycle of unsuccessful efforts to rid myself of the disorder, including time as an in-patient at St. Paul's Hospital in Vancouver, where I emerged from days of force-feeding bruised and bloated, worse than before.

Every few years, the threshold of what I would allow myself to weigh would drop a little lower, and the denial a little deeper. In the meantime, any reference to my size would leave me anxious and panicked. If the scale read one pound heavier at the end of the day, I would be scheming about how to get rid of it the next.

So now the day of reckoning has come. Years of chronic dehydration and potassium imbalance have left my kidneys little more than scar tissue. There is no one to blame. Not the system. Certainly not my family, who have painfully had to watch this unfold, nor the many doctors who tried to help me.

I am not a victim, but I do have an illness, one that dwarfs my kidney woes by a thousandfold. The truth is, this disorder's continuing grip on me is also the reason I am actually not a credible candidate for transplant. Nor would dialysis have a legitimate shot at success.

Well-meaning people in my life have suggested I should buck up and fight it. To them I gently say, I have been fighting my body for decades now and I am beyond tired.

I know what I am and where I stand. If I choose not to pretend that what I couldn't overcome in the 32 years gone by will miraculously disappear now, then so be it.

I worry, in sharing this so publicly, how my friends' and colleagues' image of me will change; how I will be judged now that my terrible weakness is exposed. I could keep this to myself and perhaps no one would be the wiser—though I know many have suspected it. I guess my reason for speaking up is because people continue to suggest I have options . . . options that for me just don't exist.

. . . .

THURSDAY, MAY 16
This is a Love Letter

This is a love letter to everyone—friends, family and people I have not met—who reached out to me today to send their love, reassurance and support for my decision to share my story. Every word you wrote helped take a bit of the shame away and for that I am eternally grateful.

But more than this, to the many people who wrote privately to share their own pain and struggles with eating disorders, or the struggles of someone they love, I thank you for the gift of your honesty and your generosity in disclosing such personal anguish.

Many people today called me "brave" and I have to say that is the last word I would use to describe myself, for it was cowardice, fear of facing the world in my own skin, and incredible self-loathing that brought me here.

More than anything, I am a cautionary tale—the embodiment of the real consequences of this abuse, and an example of how the weight of your own secrets can slowly drain the life out of your body. Perhaps it is the looming presence of my mortality that has filled me with an urgent sense that I must not let this pass without confession.

Or maybe I'm just seeking a way to make it understood what my family and the people close to me have had to contend with. This journey has cost them dearly, in so many ways. If I could spare them just a minute of this, erase every fear, false hope and disappointment, I would do it in a heartbeat.

· · · · · · · · · ·

FRIDAY, MAY 17
When the Genie Has Left the Bottle

It is the day after my disclosure, and here is another slice of truth. Several reporters have contacted me and kindly offered to "tell my story." I honestly did not contemplate the possibility of this response—though as a former reporter and communications person, perhaps I should not be surprised.

I have let them know that for now I need to let my written words speak for me. I may feel differently someday, but I am simply too shaken to contemplate exposing myself any more than I already have.

In sharing my story, it was never my intent to malign the system or the professionals who work to support those with eating disorders every day, especially since the bulk of my experiences with treatment occurred long ago. Nor do I want to draw attention to myself or put myself forward as a poster child for the afflicted.

And before letting myself off the hook, I will share with you that when the possibility of a television interview was mentioned, my very first thought was that I wasn't thin enough, and maybe I should lose a few pounds. Consider that an insight into the way this disease works. (If that seems like an illogical response, I assure you that it is rooted in legitimate concern. I remember reviewing a news story about an eating disorder patient when I worked in the Ministry of Health and the response of several of my colleagues to the patient profiled was "she doesn't look that sick." Sadly, I suspect I agreed, implying that only if her bones had been protruding through her clothes would she have earned our sympathy.)

. . . .

SATURDAY, MAY 18
What Doesn't Kill You Makes You Stronger?

The floodgates have opened and what has emerged is a river of stories that I can only describe as revelatory from both men and women—some people I thought I knew well and many I didn't. In private messages and emails, so many have come forward to send their support, and also to share stories about their own struggles with body image, or that of someone they love, in confidences so intimate that I find it hard to breathe through it.

From the beginning of my journey, with every birthday that passed, I would foolishly pray for rock bottom, because I earnestly believed that magic moment would miraculously bring me the will to get better. Well, I have found that place and while I may not be healed, something transformative is happening. Truth begets truth. The masks are coming off and with every confession, I am learning.

We are all a collection of our stories and insecurities. Stories of our childhood wounds, of the bodies that intersected with ours at some point along the road, of the voices that destroyed us and those that lifted us up. Scarred and scared on the inside, we walk through the world as if none of this damage exists. We are the walking wounded . . . but still putting one foot in front of the other.

. . . .

MONDAY, MAY 20
The Great Unknown

Sometimes I forget for minutes, or even hours, that my kidneys are failing. My mind doesn't leap on every twinge in my body thinking, "Is this a symptom? Is this the beginning of the end?" Kidney disease, it turns out, is deceptive. Because there is no real pain, it is even harder to wrap my head around the fact that there is something critically wrong. The only symptom I've had was a period when I was terribly itchy (due to a build-up of phosphorus that my body can't get rid of).

According to the specialist (and the literature) it is not a painful way to go. Most people start to sleep more and more, then slip into a coma and eventually pass away. Once I'd read that, I went through a few weeks when I was afraid to close my eyes (for obvious reasons) and when I did fall asleep, I would wake with a start every couple of hours just to reassure myself that I was still here.

While that panic has eased somewhat, I still understandably wonder when my time will come. Will I be one of those patients who hangs on for five or six years with no treatment? Or will I last through the summer? Questions no one can help me answer. For now my kidney function is said to be at around 10 per cent. As the specialist says, if we see it go down by one point a month, even I—not a wizard in math—can make that calculation! So I try to distract myself, which I suppose is a long way of explaining why writing has become so important, why I feel the need to explain how I got here and to translate some of what I am feeling into words. So I will take the uncertainty, if it means I have some time to learn from this and to wrap my arms—figuratively or otherwise—around someone else who is suffering or has suffered. I will kiss my dogs and hug my partner and smell the flowers in the garden and write like my life depends on it.

. . . .

THURSDAY, MAY 23
The Privilege of Public Service

It has been almost a year since I quit my job as director of communications with the Ministry of Health. It was a watershed moment, walking away from a job that for many years was synonymous with my life. It was said that the job was 24/7, and I took that message seriously.

Health care doesn't stop on the weekends. More often than not I was chained (by my own choice) to my phone and computer from the minute I awoke to late at night. Every day I'd receive hundreds of emails and phone calls relating tragic patient stories and myriad issues within the health-care system—a complex system in which every situation seemed to be painted in black and white by those involved. I dealt with pharmaceutical negotiations, labour issues, the black hole of seniors' care, SARS and H1N1, excessive wait times, medical errors, and families who in their grief or guilt about the loss of a loved one would lash out at the system when there was no one left to blame.

I was privileged in so many ways to be a part of that world, and with the gift of hindsight understand with a new clarity how fortunate I was to have people, right up to the end, place their trust in me. And as a patient myself, I have a new appreciation for the system I was a part of for so many years.

More significantly, I used it as an excuse to ignore what was going on with my own health—which might explain how in the six years that elapsed between doctor visits, my kidneys went from functioning to almost dead. People said I was passionate about my job, and that was true. But that can also be a kinder way of saying "strident," and I know there were many moments where I crossed the line. Still, being part of it—particularly in moments like the SARS crisis, when an entire system mobilized against an unknown enemy against a backdrop of incredible fear and uncertainty—is a privilege I will never forget.

In part, this is why I am so conflicted over my own patient journey and why I believe in my heart that pouring resources into people like me is not the answer. Not because my life doesn't have value but because I know that, as with any chronic disease, the best opportunity for healing—or at a minimum, a better outcome—comes at the beginning, not the end of the road.

. . . .

THURSDAY, MAY 23
A Perpetual State of Goodbye

I find myself in a strange limbo, on one hand hearing the ticking of an expiration clock continually in my head, and on the other hand knowing this state could, optimistically, last for years. So every communication seems to carry a weight of significance and an emotional pull that is sometimes exhausting. In some ways it is like the slate of all of your sins and misdemeanours is wiped clean and the very imperfect person you were (and are) is shrouded in a new cloak. I find it hard to recognize whom that person might be.

I am tempted to treat every interaction as though it will be my last contact with that person, my running internal commentary imploring me: "How can I possibly convey my respect and affection, or the regret I feel for every hurt I have caused?"

Every outing has to be filled with meaning. I need to find a place that feels like normal, find a way to walk in these new shoes.

Fortunately, Samuel and Daisy suffer no such dilemma. They continue to love me and occasionally shun me—as they always have done. Dogs always get it right.

. . . .

I feel this rage within me
This surging frustration
And its origin must be traced
Through my mother
Through my sisters
Through the fields of women
Picking up scraps
And being discarded
Its only target
And knives surging inward
You think I ache for you
But I ache for your power
Give it up

A Message To My 15-Year-Old Self

Dear Michelle, this may be among the hardest truths to face. This summer, you tell your mom you are going to a sleepover at your best friend's house, but you know that is a lie. Instead, you accompany her (she being your beautiful friend, who models in Vancouver from time to time) to the home of an older hockey player you are a wee bit in awe of, and whose parents are away. You know you are invited only because you are bringing that friend with you. You are a raw bundle of self-hate and insecurity, so when you get there you start drinking almost immediately.

You are not a drinker and, with the food that is not in your stomach (you starved yourself all day hoping to be stick-thin by the evening—it didn't work), you don't handle it well, not well at all. So when one of the boys marches you stumbling down the hall, where you pass out in someone's room—well, you know what comes next.

And in the early morning you wake up sick and sore, knowing what has happened and desperate to get out. You stumble home where you plaster a smile on your face and, avoiding your mom's eyes, tell her you had a nice time. The end of the story.

You will speak of it to no one but you will decide in that moment it is time to disappear, and by the next summer you will have launched that quest in earnest.

You will not in any way fathom the consequences of that choice. How it split you in two, and how all of this truth would sink further and further into the abyss, while your days of punishing yourself for that mistake—and so many others—would begin.

At some point you will almost forget how it came to this. One bad choice after another. So many reasons to keep going, until the reasons almost don't matter anymore. It is so much a part of you that it has overtaken all the reasons why. That weak, sorry girl who couldn't say no.

· · · · · · · · · ·

SATURDAY, MAY 25
A Very Public Un-Doing

What is the point of sharing all this? Dredging up ghosts, hanging them on the line in public—what possible purpose does it serve?

To be honest, I didn't intend to go this far, to a place that stops feeling brave and instead becomes something less palatable, a peep show of misery that most people would store firmly behind closed doors.

I could stop this now, and I would leave behind just a small collection of titillating tidbits; fodder for gossip that some might take as evidence that I was nothing more than a series of mistakes, bad judgment and, perhaps, rotten luck.

Of course that is not the sum of my life. But if I'm not willing to be unflinchingly honest—if I can't explain how someone who seemingly had so many advantages could land in this place, despite having a good job and people who loved and supported her—then there really is no point.

I am more than a label, a textbook definition of an illness, a case study of characteristics. On some level I am compelled to explain that there were reasons why this transpired.

Is this self-indulgence? A bid for pity? I could spare you the gory details and take them with me when I go, spare my family from revelations that cause them pain. And perhaps you think I should. I could tell you to look away, to stop reading this uncomfortable unburdening that takes me places I too would prefer to leave behind.

But that is the point. They never did go away, and the more I tried to keep them in, the more they literally ate me alive.

I need to write because it is the only way for me to control the story, to say there was more to it than this flawed surface might suggest. I write to let the ghosts go.

. . . .

SATURDAY, MAY 25
'Fun' With Numbers

Since my journey with kidney disease started, it feels like I've had more needles stuck into me than a heroin addict. In the hospital it was a daily event, which switched to weekly when I went home. We are tracking the delicate balance of minerals in the blood that nature normally regulates. In my case the results of these tests tend to produce a series of red flags as the numbers illustrate the extent of my declining kidney function.

Vaulting into the electronic age, I realized recently that I don't have to wait for a doctor's call to get the results. I can read these juicy reports myself online in real time. After all of the years I spent talking about the advent of electronic health records at the Ministry of Health, here is my opportunity to experience this system first-hand.

This development is both a blessing and a curse. While I suppose it is nice to keep an eye on how things are progressing, my reports are also a depressing read, and it is hard to look upon them with anything akin to clinical detachment. Sadly, at this point about half of the numbers on the page are outside of the "normal" range, some by a long shot.

No number fills me with more than anxiety than my GFR. In a woman my age it would normally be in the 85-90 range. As of yesterday the number was 12. Because it is calculated on averages, the specialist estimates that the true number is likely a few points lower, given my size. The worrying thing is, last week's report said 13 and so did the report before it.

Intellectually, I know it has stayed reasonably consistent for the past two months, and I shouldn't read too much into it. And yet, a part of me can't help but do just that. I wonder, when the gaps between tests stretch to a month, what that waiting will be like, where my mind will go and whether it will feel better or worse to wait another 30 days before getting a clear update on where things stand. They say knowledge is power. Sometimes I'm not so sure.

. . . .

I am not ready for love
Only a fool would think
That the prize in this lottery
Is genuine
I seek you out
And try to imagine
Why you'd even give me this night
Except you know I burn
For these temporary things
This may be the one link
We share

Iguanas and the Sands of Time

When I first met Kirk, my partner of almost 15 years, we were down at the beach drinking coffee and watching the waves go by when a man wandered into view with his pet. That might not strike you as unusual, except that in this case the pet in question was an iguana. Cue a group of Japanese students who, giggling nervously, pulled out their cameras and took endless photos while declining all invitations to actually touch said lizard (more giggling).

For months, maybe years, Kirk and I would refer to this moment in our courtship. At one point he even bought me a stuffed iguana for Christmas. Ha, ha.

Kirk's daughter Miranda reminded me today that I was 33 then, which happens to be the age she will be on her birthday in June. When I think about Miranda, it is hard to believe I could have been her age when Kirk came into my life. She seems so young, and I thought of myself as so very old then.

It was a huge leap of faith on both our parts for Kirk and I to choose to share our lives, both being wounded in various ways and not inclined to trust. The prospect of actually moving in with someone, particularly someone with a teenage daughter still at home, was daunting for me on so many levels, not the least of which was the fact I would be sharing a small space with two people who did not know about my "other life."

Of all of the people in my life, there is no one who has had a more difficult few months than Kirk. He has no escape from it—from me—and I know the future that lies ahead weighs heavily, a far different future from the one we had anticipated. He didn't sign up for this, nor any of the other revelations about my life that came out once it was too late to turn back. We have had many amazing moments, mixed with some difficult times. There were even times when we came very close to that breaking point, thinking it might be easier to go our separate ways. More than anything now, I am grateful that I am not alone. While I wish I could spare Kirk the pain that comes along with this, we are all the sum of our history. We can try to be strong for one another even when we can't be strong for ourselves.

. . . .

Too Much Information Is Not Enough

I am coming to dread seeing a certain number pop up on my BlackBerry. It is the number of my specialist's office and it generally appears in the days following my latest blood work. Today's concern is my elevated calcium and phosphorus levels. My doctors have suggested that I stop one of my current medications to see if it helps. Being me, I can't stop myself from turning to Google to see what the Internet has to say about "elevated calcium levels in patients with end-stage renal disease."

Big mistake. I zero in on an article that informs me of the highly elevated risk of death in patients with this issue. Of course I don't bother with the details—all I need is the first few lines to let my imagination go wild, convincing myself that I should have completed the advance care plan that I had been putting off last week.

There was a time when seeking this information might mean making a trip to the library and spending hours in the reference section. Not so now. We have instant access to information that can make us crazy. No car trip required. I know I shouldn't do it—nothing about these explorations makes me feel better. But like a car accident, I can't look away.

. . . .

THURSDAY, MAY 30
Three Months Ago I Was…

I got a cheque in the mail yesterday for some consulting work I'd done with some lovely people at the University of British Columbia Faculty of Medicine. I was in the early stages of what promised to be some significant work when the call came about my failing kidneys. I had to reluctantly tell my clients that I'd have to stop as I was going into hospital and I frankly didn't know what might happen next. I don't know why looking at this cheque makes me so sad—maybe because there is a part of me that wonders whether the formal part of my working life is over, or whether I'll have the strength to go back to what I love.

It also made me think about how oblivious I'd been to any warning signs that my health was in serious jeopardy. All it took was a single phone call from my doctor and nothing would ever be the same.

In early March, I was:

—pouring my heart into my contract with UBC's Faculty of Medicine and contemplating taking on more work with them,

—debating when or if I should return to a "real job," and if so, where?

—realizing that, judging from the frequent advice I was asked for, I'd learned more at the Ministry of Health than I gave myself credit for,

—still processing why I'd left my job and absorbing the lessons I'd learned through all of the difficult times; how would I do things differently in my next venture?

—missing my work colleagues more than I thought possible, and

—thinking I should really go and reconnect with my doctor. After all, it had been six years.

Of course, acting on that last point led me to where I am now—no longer blissfully ignorant about what my internal organs are up to, and thinking about the future with endless question marks.

June
2013

When the Parade Passes By

There is no sugar-coating it. I am in a slump; the kind of slump that makes the thought of putting words out there in the world a painful prospect. Every idea that flies into my head gets shot down by my own personal team of mental snipers who would prefer I just remain silent when I am feeling this way.

There are lots of reasons, and no real reason.

I am starting to feel like a bit of a bystander in my own life. I'm not strong enough to really participate; every event or activity that is even slightly more taxing than the bare minimum seems to knock me out. For the first time I can say that I am starting to feel physically like a person who has something seriously wrong going on. While this shouldn't be surprising, I think I was under the illusion it wouldn't happen quite so soon.

Then there is the sun. Anyone who knows me also knows that in the summer, I love being in the sun and am normally a nice shade of brown by July. (Yes, I know tanning is evil.) But because vitamin D is another thing my body can't process properly, I'm supposed to be avoiding it. It's petty and childish, but on a sunny week like this one, forcing myself into the shade makes me dreadfully unhappy.

Then there is the fact that Kirk is spending time with his kids in Toronto and will be heading off to Spain on Saturday, a trip I am thrilled he is taking but one I imagined we might have taken together someday.

Plus the new cabinet gets announced tomorrow, which I'll admit seems a silly thing to have on the list, but it is the first time in many years when that announcement hasn't been of direct importance to me. When you work in government, getting a new minister is transformative in so many ways, and I know all my former colleagues will be bracing for the changes that are sure to come.

In the course of a week I feel like I've shifted from being brave, cheerful and Zen-like to being sad and sick of my own thoughts. And I am so disappointed in myself for going there that hiding seems more appropriate than writing right now. To share these feelings seems the height of self-indulgence—and yet, here I am. Forcing the words out and waiting for this to pass.

. . . .

FRIDAY, JUNE 7

How Much Time Is Enough?

I read the other week about a three-year-old Salt Spring Island girl who passed away after a car accident. I thought about the special kind of hell her family must have now entered, and how every moment that passes, every special occasion, will be a reminder of her absence—the tyranny of being haunted by what might have been. It is hard for me to equate anything I am experiencing with this overwhelming loss of one so young.

Conversely, after a few days in hospital—which is increasingly the domain of the very old—one can't help but reflect upon the technological advances that can now keep us going long past our natural sell-by date. Quality of life for some of these unfortunate souls is questionable at best, and the daily indignities of helplessness reveal themselves in uncomfortable ways. Either of two inevitabilities seems to occur if you last long enough—a mind as sharp as a nail inside a body that fails to obey the simplest command, or a mind that has drifted into Neverland with a body that continues to move and twist and carry on in oblivion.

Nurses and support staff do their best with these charges, but you can feel their frustration seeping in. There are uncomfortable moments when the touch on a withered arm or the tone of voice seems a little too sharp, and the language often carries the kind of forced condescension one might use with a child who is misbehaving. I sat there thankful that during my stay I could drag my IV cart around the hallways by myself and get my own drink of water, avoiding the raw and complete dependence of my fellow patients.

Family members would show up to sit dutifully at mom's or dad's bedside, wrapped in the goodness of fulfilling a duty they didn't particularly enjoy. I imagined them ticking off a box each day with no real meaning or emotion, just registering that they'd been a good child while waiting for an end that seems like it might never come.

I think about all of this in the context of contemplating how much time is "enough" on this earthly soil. What moment constitutes "enough" before it is acceptable or natural to go? How long does one fight to carry on when the body is failing? When the body has naturally and emphatically spoken, is intervention more about what other people want?

The Art of Letting Go

When I was little I hung onto my little yellow—and ultimately frayed—blanket with a tenacity bordering on mania. My mom informs me that whenever she managed to pry it from my hands to wash it, I would stand mournfully in front of the washing machine waiting for the ordeal to end as she attempted to reassure me that it would reappear at some point.

This should be an indication of my reluctance to let go of things. Blankets, bad boyfriends, bad habits, bad jobs... I can cling on with Olympian endurance. So I find myself now struggling to come to terms with the things that I can't hang onto, and trying not to fall any further down the rabbit hole of wishing my final time away because of the things I can no longer have.

Chief among them is my work. As much as I have at times imagined stepping back into the life I once had—with a job that consumed me—my body is not up to that challenge. Unfinished business nags at me. Thoughts of opportunities I declined or failed to pursue, using my busy schedule and my slavery to incessant email as an excuse, now loom large in my consciousness. What was once avoided cannot now be reclaimed.

....

FRIDAY, JUNE 14
Karma Police

I often tell people I believe in karma—the idea that there are natural laws of justice that ensure that those who have wronged us will face retribution. Karma says that punishment is always meted out in proportion to the crime, perhaps not immediately, but in the fullness of time. What goes around comes around.

Of course, in the context of my own life, this means that I have to face the uncomfortable thought that my current state is some kind of divine comeuppance—penance for a list of previous misdemeanours. When you grow up in the Catholic faith, as I did, you become accustomed to tallying up your sins, as you never know when you might be thrust into the confessional to recite them from memory.

So I could choose to look at my current state as universal payback for the list of wrongs I keep handy. Or I could turn it around and view all of this as a cleverly disguised gift; one that allows me to feel the full weight of the love of people close to me, and many who are not so close, in the known time I have left. On any given day I find myself pondering what the karma police are saying. The jury is still out.

. . . .

> I am not of your world
> I watch you from the outskirts
> You see me cushioned in comfort
> I see you defiant and I feel your hate
> I wonder why we're together
> Why I want to feel this shame
> I want to show you what it's like
> On the other side
> I want to be inside your head
> See myself as you do
> But the only feeling we have
> Is through our fingers
> If this liquid melting into me
> Could bring our minds together
> But it only seems to tear us apart

Sunday Serenade

Sunday has always been my least favourite day of the week. From the time I was in school, the weekend for me really only covered Friday night and Saturday; Sunday was its own landscape, carrying with it all of the anticipation and often dread of the Monday that would follow.

When I was young, the Sunday night routine included watching programs such as *The Sonny & Cher Show* or *The Carol Burnett Show*. I remember being acutely aware that when the programs were over it would be time to face the torture of going to bed, my racing mind envisioning the monsters of the coming week and making them larger and nastier than could ever have been possible in real life. What had I left unfinished on Friday evening that would have to be addressed, what homework hadn't been perfectly completed? And of course, all the usual rituals would need to be endured, such as the reciting of my activities for comparison with those of friends who would casually ask, "How was your weekend?"

Sunday night, more than any other, I would find myself tossing and turning in bed and staring down the clock radio as the minutes and hours ticked by, knowing that every passing moment meant that I would have to face what lay ahead even less well rested.

After almost a year since leaving my "real" job, I still can't escape that feeling that only Sunday night can bring. I have no reason to carry the weight of this day around with me, but old habits are so hard to let go of. Which brings me to this moment— just another Sunday night, with different monsters to face.

Baby Love

There is a moment when people stop asking you whether you will ever have kids. Past a certain age, I suppose it just doesn't seem to be a relevant question anymore. But up until that point, it is a frequent topic of conversation among women, and it is one I used to get frequently.

For the most part, I would answer that I didn't know. To be honest, I never imagined that I would be very good at it. As with everything else in my life, my eating disorder was a major consideration when contemplating bringing a child into the world. While I know many women successfully navigate through a pregnancy with that affliction, it didn't seem like the best idea to me.

Nor did I relish imposing all my issues on a tiny and helpless human being who would have no option but to put up with me.

Still, I had moments when, despite all my misgivings, I couldn't help but daydream about a small but sturdy wee being who would invariably be introspective and a bit of a worrier. Sometimes a boy, but more often a girl, this phantom child would escape all the clouds hanging over my life and flourish in eternal sunshine. More realistically, she would be a flawed but hopefully resilient person who would spend her adult life working through all of the madness her mother imposed.

I saw a doctor once in my early 20s who suggested that having a baby might be the key to overcoming my eating disorder because I would be "less selfish." No doubt this would have been true. As anyone with babies knows, your life is no longer your own—a natural shift that occurs as your world tilts toward their needs.

I suppose if you have children there is comfort—and vanity—in imagining that a little piece of you will live on after you pass. My legacy, such as it is, will have to rest with the memories of people who knew me, and in the words I leave behind, all of which will naturally fade and wane with the passage of time. And in my heart, I will cradle my never-to-be baby, whose sparkling eyes will glint in the sun.

....

MONDAY, JUNE 24

A Career in Two Boxes

After almost a year of putting it off, I finally made it back to the Ministry of Health this week to pick up the two boxes I left behind when I resigned my post. They had been stored in someone's cupboard and all but forgotten until I called to say I would retrieve them.

There is nothing remarkable about their contents. Some personal items that passed for decoration in my old office; things I saved and carried with me over the years. Announcements I had worked on that held some meaning for me, clippings of news stories I'd been a part of, photographs and personal notes from staff and ministers I had worked with, a few other bits.

There are many reasons it took me this long to make the effort to take them away. Not the least of these was the false hope that I might have the option of returning someday, to pick up my life and job just where I'd left them.

Now the boxes sit unopened in our front hallway, and I find I can't bring myself to touch them, the remains of my working life.

A Burden Shared

I had a chat the other day with a former colleague who, like me, is exiled from work due to her health. It was the height of comfort to settle in with someone for whom all of the usual questions are already answered and understood.

We discussed the peculiar experience of "carrying on" with an expiration date hanging over our heads like a cramped umbrella, and laughed at how dramatically our daily routines have altered. Once accustomed to a mad whirlwind of work activity, we are now traumatized by having as many as two planned outings within a week. A casual request from our partners to pick up something for dinner must be carefully considered, as it would require actually changing out of our pyjamas and leaving the house. And our hurt feelings over being excluded from social activities are tempered by the knowledge that we would probably say no to them anyway, had we been invited.

We talked about what a watershed experience this journey can be, bringing out the most incredible love and caring from unexpected sources—and chilling silence from others with whom we confused a working relationship with friendship. It's a phenomenon I've had a lot of time to ponder in my year away.

We all need validation in unfortunate circumstances that what we are feeling and experiencing goes with the territory; a sense that we are not alone. I find myself so grateful to know that someone else has woken up this morning wondering when or if she'll change out of her bathrobe that day. A question that, for myself, I already know the answer to.

Ask me why I do it
I don't do it cause I like you
I don't do it cause I love you
I think I even hate you
But more than that
I hate myself
But you won't ask, damn it
You won't ask

· · · · · · · · · ·

SATURDAY, JUNE 29

Hunger Pains

The comic Louis C.K. has said: "The meal is not over when I'm full. The meal is over when I hate myself." This rather morbidly describes my relationship with food.

Imagine if every decision of every day where food is concerned were to trigger a stressful round of mental gymnastics. A simple discussion around going for coffee turns into a complicated negotiation—what size coffee, and will there be a temptation with that? How many calories are allowed? All day long, every day, complex calculations rage on—tallying what has already been consumed and what is likely to follow, plotting how many hours must go by before the next food battle must be fought. And then there are moments of surrender (which is always followed by panic over what has been consumed).

I have often wondered how much of my energy has gone toward trying to maintain a semblance of normalcy, and what I might have done with it had it been directed toward something useful.

Of course you learn very quickly that none of this is really about food. It is the symptom of a different problem, and yet the symptom never goes away.

I imagine heroin addicts or alcoholics must feel constantly dogged by the feeling that their drug of choice is always within reach, or just beyond it. Addiction is a difficult dragon to slay, but addicts who successfully overcome it will find that it's quite possible to live and breathe without both of those substances, and even to avoid situations in which they are present.

Not so with food.

Food is the unending temptation. There is not a moment of the day in our food-obsessed culture when people aren't actively anticipating their next meal, analyzing the meal they just had or dreaming about what they might consume in the future.

If you strip all pleasure out of the experience of eating, what you are left with is a feeling on the other side of normal—and a raw, gnawing hunger for some kind of peace, a hunger that could consume the moon.

July

2013

Of Mice and Men

I watched a news story the other day about scientists who used stem cells to create mini-livers from scratch that were later implanted in mice and worked like a charm. The announcer blithely commented that this raises the prospect that soon they will be able to create all sorts of organs, implying that it's as easy as dumping a few random cells into a Petri dish and letting them work their magic.

Imagine a world in which those with organ failure can step up to a butcher-like counter and proclaim, "I'll have one heart, a kidney... and is the liver on special today?" What a wonderful world.

Of course, as is typical of this type of report, many things are glossed over. They don't talk about the incredible resources and time it would take to get to that point, the inevitable complications and failures along the way, who is paying the bills (which can always influence the outcome in the research community) and the huge moral and ethical questions this raises.

Every medical advance assumes there is a willing group of taxpayers anxious to ante up and embrace new technology and procedures, no matter how flimsy the outcome and no matter how old, infirm or "non-compliant" the patient might be.

The reality is that most of our hospital beds now are taken up by the very old; people for whom medical advances perform the task of extending, rather than improving, life.

I suppose there is a part of me that internally shouts "hurrah" at these medical innovations. Redemption is possible for me and my failing kidneys, with virtually no work on my part.

But are we all meant to be here forever, recycling ourselves and creating new body parts to replace the old, ignoring our natural life cycle and Botoxing our way to eternity?

I suppose for some people the answer is yes, one thousand times yes. And if the opportunity for a Petri-dish kidney transplant was real, I suspect I would be sorely tempted, in my current situation. Everything else might fall to pieces, but my shiny new kidneys would do the job they were intended to do, and I would be like a mouse on a treadmill, running as fast as I can.

. . . .

WEDNESDAY, JULY 17

40 Winks... Please

When I was a little girl, it was part of our nightly routine to say our prayers. One prayer included the lines: "If I should die before I wake, I pray the Lord my soul to take," a rather gruesome sentiment for a child to revisit on a daily basis.

Being a kid with an active imagination and a born worrier, I couldn't help wondering what circumstances might strike in the dead of night to whisk me away. Was there some epidemic of middle-of-the-night child deaths I was not aware of? And where exactly would my soul go?

This internal dialogue, that inner voice that chatters incessantly as soon as my head hits the pillow, is one of the reasons why sleep is not my friend.

While I have spent many hours over the years checking the clock radio to gauge just how long I have been sleepless, I used to be able to make up for some of that lost time by taking long and delicious naps on weekend afternoons, when somehow it didn't take much effort to succumb. Now, naps seem impossible.

When I worked in radio, I did the early-morning shift for several years, which involved dragging myself into the station around 4:30 a.m. In order to have any kind of a life in the evening, afternoon naps were an absolute necessity. I would often wake up with a start on a dark winter afternoon, look at the clock and be convinced I was late for work—even getting halfway to the parking lot before realizing my error.

I walked around in a state of near-constant sleep deprivation throughout that time. You soon come to recognize what a profound effect that sweet respite has on your view of the world. That moment of fading to black, embracing the nothingness, the inner voice mercifully quiet, waiting for the sun.

. . . .

THURSDAY, JULY 18
If You Can't Say Anything Nice...

Honesty is tough. It requires a lot of effort to look at where you are and admit that you've descended into a dark place, to acknowledge it and to try to figure out how to climb out of it with a modicum of grace.

I was naïve, when I started this journey, to think that it would be a straight shot from diagnosis to the end. I imagined that I would stand somewhat aloof from everything that was happening, accepting the inevitable and watching the process with the detachment of an anthropologist observing the habits of a Pygmy tribe.

Of course there is no detachment, though in retrospect the initial shock seemed to buffer me from the full realization that everything has shifted. Initially, everything sounded more imminent, in part because there was no real baseline to compare my situation to. But over the last four months, nothing has really changed from a clinical perspective and it has left me perplexed and anxious about what I am supposed to do now. And from there I landed in a space where I wanted to stand on the edge of the ocean and scream into the wind until my voice had left me.

Seeing other people moving forward and living their lives— even in the very smallest moments and experiences—filled me with a deep and profound resentment. In a nutshell, I felt intensely and utterly sorry for myself, which is a very nasty feeling indeed.

It is hard to confess that I felt that way because I feel a deep need to do this "right"—to be cheery and Zen-like—not to lose perspective or let myself drown in self-pity.

I know the resentment is not really directed toward anyone else, but more to the lack of control I feel over how my future might unfold. And I feel a simmering anger toward myself for not being strong enough to prevent this in the first place. So the only way I know how to get over this is to stop putting off the things I need to do to get my proverbial house in order, sort out the things I can control and drag myself out of inertia.

It is a slow and painful climb, and if adversity is a great teacher then it is time for those lessons to kick in.

THURSDAY, JULY 25
Just a Spoonful of Sugar

I love my specialist. His discussions with me are direct and unflinching, but couched in warmth and compassion. Every patient deserves to feel that the white coat on the other side of the desk is your advocate, even when the answers don't come easy or are hard to hear.

We've come to a place where the road forward is pretty clearly defined, but the timing less so. When we met this week, among the topics of our conversation was our mutual dislike of big pharmaceutical companies and the gouging that takes place when patients are at their most desperate. As a case in point, he suggested that if I was "independently wealthy" (which I am not!) I could take a medication that costs $1,000 per month to help control my phosphorus levels, as the simple calcium supplements haven't been working. There are other options, including surgical intervention to remove the parathyroid glands that are causing the problem in the first place, but we aren't at that point now.

It is a stark reminder that even in our generous public healthcare system, somehow the profiteers still find ways to make a buck with add-ons that seem just out of reach.

When I worked in the Health Ministry we saw many cases of patients advocating through the media for coverage of new, experimental or prohibitively expensive medications that were not covered through our provincial drug plan, and they always inspired heated discussions. I always wondered why people directed their vitriol at the ministry when the stories that would often emerge were of drug companies holding the patients for ransom, often by starting them off on free samples for a year or so and then cutting them off when they were entirely dependent. Often these drugs were for conditions so rare that no reasonable research exists to prove whether or not they actually work, as adequate sample sizes just don't exist. Still, the political pressure in these cases is enormous and the drug companies never seem to take the heat. As a patient, it is natural to want to find the latest pill to take your symptoms away, but in my experience, some pills are simply too hard to swallow.

. . . .

MONDAY, JULY 29
Vacation in a Box

I did something completely ridiculous the other day. I ordered a swimsuit online.

It's not the swimsuit itself that's ridiculous—it's that I don't swim. At least, I haven't since I was a kid (not counting water aerobics, which was an obsession for awhile some years ago). Suddenly, the thought of immersing myself in a pool brought on an urge so powerful that some part of me decided this swimsuit was an essential purchase.

This is no mere bathing suit. Oh, no. Technically, it is a triathlete outfit. I only picked it because it covers the maximum amount of skin possible short of a full wetsuit—which of course would really be madness!

Apparently it is hurtling toward me as I write this. And I can say with complete confidence that the chance of me actually using it for the purpose intended is zero. In fact, my communion with a pool under any circumstances is at this point highly unlikely. Nevertheless, the thought of it makes me deliriously happy—like a vacation will soon be delivered to my door.

You could call it an impulse purchase, and on one level it most certainly is. But on another level it feels somehow necessary to have this costume—the garb of a healthy person, who might sport it while cycling around the city or crossing a lake.

Every activity feels more and more taxing these days, and my expectations about how each day might unfold are continually contracting. There is something about the idea of plunging into a pool of warm water—feeling my body rise up from the deep end, weightless and unanchored, floating to the surface for that first breath of air—that is calling to me. So I wait for my parcel to appear, to tear open the box and let the magic out.

August
2013

TUESDAY, AUGUST 6
Buyer Beware!

The new triathlete suit arrived today, concealed in a Purolator envelope. Huzzah! I ripped open the wrapping to find a black, hot pink and white nylon piece of fabric with a zipper down the front. How stylish! How flattering it was sure to be.

We (by "we" I mean me and my new suit) hurried upstairs to try it on.

That was 20 minutes ago, which is precisely how long it took me to squeeze into it. If I did not already have organ damage, I can assure you, I have now. It probably didn't help that I was laughing so hard.

I do not know what kind of stick insect this item was meant to house, but I can assure you it was not me. So my dreams of deep water are temporarily on hold while I contemplate another option. Perhaps a tent with armholes.

Don't Ask, Don't Tell

Please don't ask me how I feel.

If I answer that question honestly, I will make you feel bad, and that will make it worse.

My body is becoming a toxic soup. Surely you can see, as I see in my own eyes, this slow decline . . . this shutting down.

I could tell you I feel fine. And honestly, I do try to say it out loud. But you know and I know it is not the truth. If I say that I feel a little better today, it's only to help you avoid something you don't want to face right now.

I need to be able to tell you that I am not OK. Not for your sympathy, but for the sweet release of not having to push myself to try to keep up with a semblance of normal right now. I need to allow myself to be where I am.

How do I feel? I feel like sorting through my clothes and getting rid of everything except the very few things that make me comfortable. Ditto the shoes, the many purses, anything that represents the life I am not living.

How do I feel? I feel hot and feverish, and I am losing sensation in my toes. My stomach feels like acid all the time, and I wake up with a taste like the sour metal of a gun in my mouth, a taste that does not leave me.

How do I feel? I feel like saying nothing but "I am sorry" and "I love you"—it is all that really seems necessary.

How do I feel? I feel like throwing away anything that would remind you of me, any trace that I was here. I feel like crawling under the sheets with my books around me on the bed, and just staying there.

I am sore and sad and scared, and anything but at peace. I am jammed full of places to go and no way to get there. I am—to borrow from Marian Engel—as sharp as a bed of nails an Indian swami would lie down on.

How do I feel? I am remembering everything that ever happened and seeing it spoil before my eyes, like it was too much or never enough. Like someone has stopped the music and there is no chair left for me to rest on.

How do I feel? Afraid to send this into the universe, and afraid not to.

So, how do I really feel? OK, but more importantly, how are you?

....

SUNDAY, AUGUST 11
Midnight at the Oasis

The thing about my current state is that often I don't know where the symptoms of my kidney failure end and other things begin. That is why, after a particularly miserable day, I found myself heading to the emergency room yesterday.

It is difficult for me to give in and admit I need help, and I was woefully apologetic to the hard-working staff who were spending a long Saturday night caring for a roomful of walking wounded with all manner of ailments. There is very little privacy in that environment and one can't help but pick up the stories of fellow inmates, many of whom were awaiting consults with psychiatric staff for one reason or another, or cuddling wee ones wearing their misery on their sleeves.

Fortunately I had a very short wait, and before very long I was in a stretcher with some fluids and an IV antibiotic, which made me feel much better. The ER doctor was funny, kind and compassionate. Sensing I was feeling low, he popped out of the consult room and came back with my chart from my hospital stay in March. He flipped to a sheet in the middle of the file on which my specialist had written notes, and asked if I could read the handwriting. Trepidatious about what it might say, I tried but couldn't make it out, so he read it to me: "48-year-old female—delightful," which made me smile.

I thought about the fact that comment was written by my specialist on the day he had informed me my kidneys were dying, and of all the impressions I might have left in that tiny room, that is the word he used to describe me. I wondered about the version of me that doctor had seen, why it felt so far removed from the me that I know, and whether it was possible to believe in that part of myself.

Six hours later I was home, grateful to be in my bed and feeling so much better than I had when I arrived at the hospital. I am starting to understand that choosing "comfort measures" over treatment doesn't mean suffering—and that I am entitled to alleviate the little things, even if the big things remain as they are.

· · · · · · · · · ·

MONDAY, AUGUST 19
Call in the Fat Police

There are many things that public health officials do well, but every now and then a line is crossed where some well-meaning initiatives go a step too far.

This is what is happening in Toronto, where public schools are taking it upon themselves to start weighing kids as part of their war on obesity. They claim this is based on a successful American model. But as a former pudgy kid, I can tell you that no one needed to send me a letter or weigh me in front of my peers to clue me in to the fact that I was overweight. I was the poster child for body humiliation. No outsider could possibly have matched the disapproval I already felt for my own shape.

Kids never let you forget it when you don't measure up—and it's easy to see how annual advertising campaigns featuring paper-thin children in their back-to-school garb must only feed this intolerance. I've been seeing ads lately from Joe Fresh, promoting skinny cords as part of their back-to-school-shopping cash grab. I think of the 12-year-old girls and boys everywhere whose bodies will never, ever look like that, no matter how many meals they skip or apples they eat.

There is not a single model in those campaigns who in any way compares to the unhappy teenage shoppers who will leave those stores with their hopes dashed, hating their bodies with a depth I can't possibly put into words. So, back off, fat police—and why not contemplate the power of self-respect?

. . . .

WEDNESDAY, AUGUST 21

A Stitch in Time

Many people lament and debate the rising cost of health care, the looming human resource shortages that could leave many baby boomers scrambling for care. But with my own recent exposure to the health-care system I can say with confidence that the greatest gifts my family doctor and nephrologist have given me are their time and their unfailing compassion. I have never for a moment felt like a nuisance in their presence, never felt like my questions, concerns or secrets weren't treated with the utmost reverence or respect. It is not the interventions, equipment or devices that give me comfort—it is their consistent and embracing care.

At its current convention, the Canadian Medical Association spent a lot of time discussing end-of-life care but stopped short of a discussion about physicians aiding patients in their choices in those critical moments. I truly wonder why we are so loath to contemplate it, when we freely accept veterinarians putting our beloved pets out of their misery when they are suffering and in pain.

It is not just a question of the exorbitant resources we expend as a society in a patient's final years (and it is a fact that the greatest health-care costs accompany the last 10 to 15 years of our lives). What concerns me is the notion that we should accept the suffering that these interventions entail as a good thing. Families often push for more in their guilt and grief. I don't think any reasonable discussion about end-of-life care can ignore a patient's right to say they have had enough—and it is cowardice that prevents us from tackling a discussion about how and when easing someone into the light is acceptable.

. . . .

THURSDAY, AUGUST 22

A Risk Too Far?

I had a unique experience yesterday, when I went for the third appointment to deal with a painful twist in my back. I don't quite know how to say this, but I got the distinct impression that the physiotherapist would prefer I not come back. He didn't say it outright, to be fair, but the way he emphasized that it would be OK for me to cancel my next appointment left me with that feeling.

I gather that for liability purposes, treating someone like me is a bit daunting as my bones are quite frail and of course the pain in my kidneys likely makes me difficult to treat. Right now it is almost back in alignment and I can stand upright—which was an impossibility on the weekend—so that is good. I am trying to faithfully do the exercises he gave me, but in an ironic twist, disturbing the muscles this way releases creatinine, which makes my kidneys worse.

This experience has made me think about windows closing, and whether some professionals will be uncomfortable in helping me as this progresses, and then where will I be? I know if I really needed it my doctors would do their best to help, but there was something quite humiliating about that moment at the physiotherapist's office. It makes me think about dignity, and how much you lose when you are at the mercy of other people for their help—something I still find very hard to embrace or accept.

I know these are all lessons that on some level I need to learn—and I have empathy for the therapist, who I'm sure didn't want to cause me harm.

"Healing," or what passes for it, is a complicated affair, and right now I just have to breathe deeply and hope it is not too soon before I find myself looking for those particular helping hands again.

. . . .

> I'm shrinking from your out-stretched fist
> But you are my tool
> To chip away this façade
> And mould my body
> Into something resembling
> My vision of myself
> We contribute to this ugliness
> You are the mirror
> Reflecting an image
> I've created

Why

I've always been much more afraid of living than dying.

This might help explain why I am not fighting to hang on the way I know many people in my position passionately try to do.

To be honest, I never felt like I really got the hang of it that well—living, I mean. I started off with a lot of lost things, and I suspect those gaping holes just never got filled back up.

I was always too worried, too afraid of who I was and how the world perceived me. There was nowhere to hide from it, and seemingly no way to feel OK in my skin.

Of course, this is not to say there weren't happy moments, but I couldn't quite get the knack of sustaining peace without punishing myself. Finally that punishment was so deeply ingrained that it became part of a tired routine that I just couldn't shake. I don't know what could have changed it—I've had many people in my life who genuinely cared about me—but none of it seemed to reach the core of my own perceptions. It is why I believe so passionately that to beat this disorder, the right kinds of tailored interventions have to happen early, and be sustained for as long as it takes.

This does not mean locking people away to live in some kind of treatment bubble with all of their choices prescribed by somebody else, only to be thrust back into the same environment that landed them in trouble in the first place. (Though I admit that, medically speaking, there are times when a hospital stay or residential treatment program is necessary.) But my short-lived experience with being an in-patient for my eating disorder meant days of being pumped full of fluids and food my body simply could not adequately absorb after years of denial. I would go home such an anxiety-stricken mess, I made sure all of that "progress" was eliminated as soon as I could possibly manage it.

Out-treatment for me was a government-funded program with the majority of facilitators offering no real insight or expertise. The final straw was when my own "counsellor" suggested drinking as an alternative.

I say all this knowing that there was a part of me for which it was too late even before treatment began. While I do believe people can change, there was a stubborn, unmoving part of me that wasn't prepared to face the consequences of giving up what I knew, however harmful it was, and having to cope with this life without my deeply flawed safety net.

It is only human to seek some external force that might succeed in relieving us of problems like this—some professional or group who can flip an internal switch for us and make it all go away. But to let it go, it takes an incredible force of one's own will and a sense that you are valuable enough to be worth saving.

Having been on the inside of government, I can say that patient advocacy is generally perceived as an attack. Public servants literally jump in their defensiveness to protect what they've budgeted for and the policies they have created. So instead of standing on a soapbox, I will simply say that, regardless of what was or wasn't available to me, I now know that the only real tool worth giving to young people at risk is a sense of their own self-worth, and an unassailable belief that, regardless of the challenges they face, they are worth fighting for.

Suffer the Children

I had to pick up a prescription the other day and, because it was going to be a bit of a wait, I decided to pass the time by getting a coffee. While I was standing in line I noticed a woman, not young, not old, but exceptionally thin, rifling through a rack of newspapers and magazines before circling the store in an agitated way. She picked up almost every item on the display shelves as if she was desperately searching for something, then crouched on the ground, contemplating what was in her hands.

It was clear that she was not there to make a purchase and, further, it was clear that she was either mentally ill and off her medication, or high on something other than life. I noticed many of my fellow patrons either openly watching her with narrowed eyes and pursed lips, or stealing glances at her as she moved around the store.

I asked the staff (who had been taking turns stepping out from behind the counter to watch her) whether they thought she needed medical attention. Their response was that she was "in there all the time" and that mostly, they tried to keep an eye on her.

While I was having this conversation, she walked out of the store. I didn't see her again. I don't know where she went, or if she even had anywhere to go. I don't know if anyone cared that she was on her own and extremely vulnerable.

It was one of those situations that makes you feel wholly helpless, despite any good intentions. I wouldn't know where to begin to intervene, or if inserting myself would do any good. It left me feeling unsettled for the rest of the day, like a puzzle that cannot be solved, even when a life depends upon it.

A Poem is My Prescription

It is rare for a doctor to prescribe a poem as part of the healing journey, and yet that is among the things my lovely family doctor recommended during my last visit. As you might have gathered by now, we have a very special relationship, and one that I have come to treasure more acutely in recent months.

She described how her family had gone through a terrible tragedy and talked about a poem by Irish writer John O'Donohue that related to the "interim" period—a time after some significant life event (diagnosis) when the foundations of your life have been torn away and you need to find a path to adjust to a new set of realities. The poem, *For the Interim Time*, describes how difficult and slow it is "to become new," but promises, "The more faithfully you can endure here/The more refined your heart will become/For your arrival in the new dawn." It is not only beautiful, but also perfectly describes where I am.

September
2013

THURSDAY, SEPTEMBER 5

Close Encounters

It is probably inevitable that because my house and the nearest grocery store/drugstore/coffee shop are within walking distance of the legislature that I run into people from my former life, both people I worked with at one time or knew as acquaintances. Some ignore me entirely—purposefully or not—while others are generally friendly and ask how I am doing. It is expected now for some part of these exchanges to include some sizing up—which is not surprising, knowing how far news about my health situation spread—their eyes summing up my current physical state. It is very much a part of a normal human response to be curious when you meet a person like me in the flesh.

It fills me with such a nervous, self-conscious feeling, so bad that if I have the energy I'll drive for miles to a drugstore where such an encounter is less likely. I know it is silly to feel so undone, and of course there are faces I miss. It's not that I'm not happy to see them, but what I am afraid of is the feeling that they are seeing something my eyes will not let me see, some visible decay that careful preparation cannot hide.

It's not that they would say it, but I would know it instinctively—the discomfort it might inspire—from the look in their eyes, the tilt of their heads.

I am genuinely trying to push past this, knowing we all have our good and bad days, the times we might prefer not to be seen, and to focus on the caring, not the curiosity, that might lie behind the smile. To recall what I appreciated about that person who inhabits a world I used to dwell in in my working life, but where I no longer live.

. . . .

FRIDAY, SEPTEMBER 6
Sabotage

There are times I think there are things I just shouldn't share, as it doesn't exactly cast me in a favourable light. But it is all part of the human experience, so onward I go.

Yesterday, in an effort to get out of the house, I decided to take a quick trip to the store. The driveway was wet and my stupid foot shot out from under me, ankle bashed car on the way down, I scraped a large patch on my arm and, worst, I landed on my hip bone, where I now have a growing welt. I have also wrenched the same twisted part of my back that was trying to heal.

When it happened I just lay there like an idiot on the pavement in the driveway in shock before hobbling up and back to the house. I then confess I cried like a baby a) because it hurt like hell and b) because I had been walking around so gingerly all week, trying so hard to be OK and c) I am supposed to be leaving tomorrow morning for my first weekend out of town since well before my diagnosis.

I am beyond questioning why these things are happening when I was trying so hard to stay on track. You see, the last time we had planned such a weekend getaway was two days before I landed in the hospital and had to cancel everything. So I was determined nothing would mar this and there is nothing left now but to try to have faith that I can push through.

Was it self-sabotage or just a klutzy moment that could happen to anyone? It doesn't really matter now—it has happened and I have about 24 hours to try to get past this. More than anything I feel bad for Kirk, who needed a drama-free escape as much or more than I do and all of my apologies can't take away the fact that we have added a little unwelcome weight to our shoulders at a time when we really could do without it.

. . . .

SUNDAY, SEPTEMBER 8

Dear Body

Dear body, I am begging you now, please try to co-operate.

You are behaving like a petulant child, flopping off in every direction and defying any effort I seem to make to follow the specialist's advice and get out into the world and do things "while you still can."

I am beginning to hate that sentiment—the notion that there is yet another list of things I have to do in order to say that I am following the process like I should. I keep telling myself there must be some purpose to this, some lesson in patience, humility or acceptance that I need to learn. My mind keeps making plans—simple or grand schemes—and my body will have none of it. I guess I punished it and it is punishing me right back.

Or maybe the fact that my body is stealing my focus means that it is necessary. Feeling the pain is one way not to let my mind wander to the myriad places it can't stay away from and the questions that no one can answer with any certainty.

Instead of jumping ahead to one million different scenarios around how the future will unfold, it grounds me here, in this place, gingerly contemplating the best way to get up from a chair with the least physical discomfort. Forces me to see things that I could not see before, and appreciate how far people have been willing to extend themselves to help me and to will me good things, even if those good things do not come.

It is enough to make me want to rip up the pity party favours that I have so amply handed myself, stop making plans I can't pursue and just lean into this life I have, which for now has to be enough—and is in so many ways, more than I ever expected.

· · · · · · · · · ·

TUESDAY, SEPTEMBER 10

Nine to Five

It is a common enough question: "Where do you work?" Since I was 15, I always had an answer to that.

My first official job was as a hostess at a Chinese restaurant where the kitchen staff only spoke Cantonese, and the waitresses were surly and complained bitterly when I sat some hungry family in their section. As a bonus they let me take home the broken fortune cookies for free.

These days, simple things like being asked for my work phone number by a clerk inspires a panic in me. What if this complete stranger finds out I have no position and heaps all sorts of judgments upon me? It's clear from looking at me that I am not an heiress. If work defines us, as it so often does in our society, who are we when we are not gainfully employed? What are we but a drain on an otherwise productive landscape where everyone is busily getting ahead?

The struggle to identify what remains of me now that that critical piece of my identity has been shelved is a puzzle I continue to try to piece together, all the while wistfully dreaming that I might return to that place of certainty. That costume that may be ill-fitting now, but it is familiar nonetheless.

· · · · · · · · · ·

TUESDAY, SEPTEMBER 10
I Wish I Had a River I Could Skate Away On

When I hear Joni Mitchell sing those words, to borrow her own lyrics, I feel weak in the knees. I know it is a cold weather kind of song, but for some reason it sprang into my head today while I was paying my first visit to the acupuncturist.

I have never really had occasion to explore complementary medicine, but I am making up for it now. With my face squished into the doughnut-like pillow on the treatment table, waiting for the magic to happen, I was trying desperately to still my thoughts and be peaceful, although I find that a challenge at the best of times.

The relief I felt was immediate and striking, even if my mind didn't really want to co-operate. I am so grateful that I can pursue some of these options, even for a short time. The search for something resembling healing and the business of juggling appointments is a taxing one, and you never really know what you will find. When it actually works, it is like some kind of miracle. Still, sometimes all you really want to do is skate away to some other place and time—to escape the need to heal, and to feel relief in the mind as well as in the body.

I hear your voice
And Need No Clues
But we play this guessing game
anyway
You lead me into the questions
And I oblige
But I try not to make it easy
We pretend there's some foundation for this
Though we never scratch this surface
You're still wondering how far you can push me
I wonder how far I can be pushed
You believe there's more I can give you
But you're not sure whether you want it
This creeping desperation
Makes you say things you don't believe
We bring out the worst in each other
Because even through this petty discourse
We hear the truth

. . . .

SUNDAY, SEPTEMBER 15
Tipping the Scales

When one person in a relationship becomes dependent on the other, the ground shifts and new roles have to be forged, tipping the balance in a new direction. Every petty frustration or resentment of the past pales in comparison to this new emotional territory.

As a person accustomed to grabbing the reins, I find it a painful process to give up the power to steer—the blessing and curse of being in control. When you are not responsible for a task, you lose the right to criticize others for how they choose to perform it—or so they say. In practice, this is not so easy to stick to.

Sometimes I feel like I should just wander off like a wounded animal, curl up into a ball and let the herd carry on without me. These are the places my mind goes to when I am brutally honest, on days when the business of not shouldering my share of the load becomes too great a weight to bear, and my apologies for this fact seem hollow.

Then a good day comes when it is almost possible to believe this chasm does not exist—when I can feel my own power, and a glimpse of what I once had shines through. An imperfect picture, but preferable to this new normal...this limping gait that I just can't get the hang of.

. . . .

THURSDAY, SEPTEMBER 19
Love, Love, Love

I've been thinking a lot about love—sharing it, withholding it, tossing the word around lightly.

Since my diagnosis I share that word a lot more. I say it with emphasis, a sense of urgency, as though it is imperative that people understand to the depth of their being how much they mean to me. I find myself wanting to take people by the hand, look them square in the eye and not turn away from whatever response might lie there.

There is still a sliver within me that balks at this new connectedness, something I actively steered clear of in the past. My instinct has always been to question in the most cynical way the intention behind the sentiment, instead of accepting it freely and purely for what it was.

I know that my current state has an effect on people's reactions, creating a kind of distorted reality in which positive qualities are unnaturally heaped upon a deeply flawed and normal human life. Perhaps the eyes that look upon me, now that I have bared my soul, see only this new construct—this glass house that I have created. Yet I can't help feeling that I might have missed these gifts, had things unfolded differently. The love I have received from the people who have reached out to me over the past six months is a rare and precious thing—and perhaps their motivation is less important than the glow they leave behind.

. . . .

FRIDAY, SEPTEMBER 20

The Old Grey Mare, She Ain't What She Used To Be

I haven't gone out much lately, but when I found the walls closing in today I decided the only antidote was shopping.

I'll admit I have always loved to shop. I am decisive about it; no dithering. I walk into a store, peruse the merchandise as if I'm being timed in a road-race, and with a glance can see exactly what I like and don't like. I handle it like a reconnaissance mission: assess the territory and strike.

But shopping feels different now. First, because I am increasingly conscious of my dwindling bank balance and second, because a part of me wonders why I would invest in a single new item when I literally have racks of clothes I do not wear anymore. The morbid part of me looks at it as one more piece of irrelevant merchandise that someone in my life will have to bag up and dispose of at some point—a thought I desperately tried to push from my mind as I drove.

The items I seek out are different now. I find myself searching for comfort; soft fabric that will not chafe, anything to bring me warmth.

This is how I found myself under the unforgiving lights of a dressing room today, forced to confront my own face in the mirror, still looking for signs of my current state that I may have missed before. Perhaps the bored salesperson might pick up on these clues and look at me as something other than just another older woman trying on clothes that are likely too young for her. I don't know why I care. What I see is really no different from what I have always seen—someone playing dress-up and trying to be anyone but who she is.

· · · · · · · · · ·

TUESDAY, SEPTEMBER 24

Forget Your Troubles, Come On Get Happy

I have had a lot of happy news lately from people in my life who are celebrating some of life's bigger moments—a former colleague who goes on maternity leave this week awaiting her first baby, another who just got engaged. My excitement over all of the upcoming events has me floating, brimming with the fullness of their joy.

In my latest lab work, my numbers had perked up a bit—not better than when my kidney issues were first discovered, but better in some areas than they had been in a while. I never know what I will discover each month when I go online and peek, my eyes half-closed, at the numbers that tell me where I have landed. I couldn't help thinking that this wave of events and announcements—the happiness I feel on my friends' behalf—has had a positive influence on my health.

At the same time, each piece of good news brings with it a twinge of something darker. It is impossible now not to regard events that will occur in the future with a question mark, some sting of uncertainty about where I will be, what state I might find myself in, when these happy occasions take place.

It is also forcing me to acknowledge that life marches on. It doesn't stop to suit my mood or is in any way diminished by my standing still. For now, all I want to do is focus on the forward movement. I still have a front-row seat on all the action—not quite a participant, but an enthusiastic cheerleader for the people I love, their initiations into the next phase of life and the new beginnings that peek around the next corner.

. . . .

TUESDAY, SEPTEMBER 24
A Matter of Life and Death

Dr. Donald Low, a leading light in the field of public health, has died, leaving behind an impassioned plea for physician-assisted suicide as part of his legacy. Dying of a brain tumour, he worried about the manner in which he would die—a feeling that I can certainly identify with at this stage of the game.

My specialist and others have told me that in many ways I am lucky. Given many alternatives, they say dying of kidney failure is not particularly painful. They describe it almost like a descent into hibernation—you grow sleepier and sleepier, until the final deep sleep comes. But I still feel the need to believe I will have some control over that—that we all deserve the opportunity to decide how the story ends.

I know some people have strong and valid arguments against this idea, for religious or other reasons, including the possibility that people may prematurely take advantage of this freedom to choose.

My feelings on the topic are not secret and yes, they are clouded by my own self-interest.

I know that I can have a care plan that lays out when and if medical intervention will take place—and maybe that sounds like another way of expediting the process—but that plan is only focused on the extraordinary measures that might have been taken to keep me alive, not those that might ease me into the light.

Our discomfort with this topic is understandable, but I think it is time we got over it and accepted that at a minimum, we need to talk. It shouldn't take a leading physician staring death in the face to wake us up to this conversation.

···········

WEDNESDAY, SEPTEMBER 25
This Magic Moment

I had a message today from someone I worked with back in 2003, who had read these pages and took the time to brighten my day with a note.

She recalled that way back in the day, when sadly her own dad was dying of lung cancer, I had stepped into her office and offered to help out by doing some grocery shopping for her, or anything else she needed—a gesture that had in all honesty slipped from my memory, but that she had never forgotten.

My intention in repeating this story is not to cast either of us in any particular light, but to emphasize the tremendous impact that what we say, or do not say, can have on a person who is struggling to keep a brave face in the midst of some personal turmoil.

In putting my story out there for the world to see, warts and all, I continue to be given the most magical gifts—surprising, and often overwhelming, disclosures from special people I have met on this journey.

I could equally tell you a story of someone who might not remember me in such a fond fashion—and that is a burden I suspect we all have to carry. But for today, I will take this gem and contemplate the power of a gesture, however small, and this new world of miracles that continues to knock on my door.

....

THURSDAY, SEPTEMBER 26
No Place Like Home

For someone who hasn't had a great deal going on other than appointments and ER visits, I seem to have a significant number of new and pending developments this week. The first is that I am fleeing Victoria tomorrow (and I am serious this time) for the shiny metropolis of Toronto, for a quick visit with some of the people I love most.

Second, we took the plunge and met with a realtor about finally putting our beloved house on the market, which could happen within just a few weeks by the look of things. It was a necessary decision, but one that makes me emotional at the same time.

I was a very late bloomer when it came to real estate. This is the second place we (and the bank!) have owned, after years of schlepping from rental to rental. While Kirk had previously known the joy and pain of home ownership, it was all new to me. We started with a townhouse. Later, when things were looking up in our careers and the market was at its peak, we set our sights on this small, tucked-away house in James Bay.

But time and circumstances have changed since then, and making a shift to something more manageable is necessary now, for all sorts of reasons. The prospect of moving on carries a lot of excitement mixed in, for me, with a bit of sorrow.

I resist change of all kinds. I crave it constantly, but when it comes down to it, I am usually either too afraid or too resigned to leap.

I think about our youngest dog-child; this is the only home she has ever known. The prospect of taking both of our pups away from a neighbourhood they love makes me teary-eyed. And the fact is, this place is so much more than a house to me. It has been my shelter, and a symbol of everything I worked for and thought I needed to achieve.

But as I started to load up my suitcase this morning, I thought about the things that are essential—the things we carry with us, and those we leave behind. When you get right down to it, what we really need is so much less than what we think we want, and the baggage we can't let go of is so much bigger than our shoulders need to bear.

October
2013

SATURDAY, OCTOBER 5

The Bare Necessities

Decluttering is not for the faint of heart. It requires a certain grit and determination, the kind employed by those brave souls who do things like enter Iron-Man competitions or give birth.

I find myself wearily walking past my closet several times a day, peeking in to see if by some miracle the contents have sorted themselves out. But no, it is all still there—mountains of items that at one time I just "had to have," and which have hung there un-worn and un-loved for months or, in some cases, years.

Yesterday I filled three huge bags with items to be donated, which barely made a dent in the collection. It's the same story in our kitchen, with its shelves lined with items meant for the enter-taining we rarely do, and the crawl space, which is filled with boxes whose contents have not seen the light of day since we moved into this house. Mountains of random, miscellaneous material that we have carried with us from place to place. What is wrong with this picture?

The sad thing is, we are the type of people who routinely put our items out for collection when groups like the Diabetes

Association come around, so this current mass of merchandise is but a fraction of what we have already discarded.

I vow with this move—as I do with every move—that this time, things will be different. We will be ruthless, emotionally detached, singing "you can't take it with you" as we sift through it, drawer by drawer, closet by closet, until nothing but what really matters remains.

But tackling my clothes closet has been more of an emotional roller-coaster than I anticipated. I put items into the donate bag, only to take them out again, and put them back in, and so on, dozens of times before steeling myself to finally and eternally let them go.

Rolling through the back of my mind is the central gnawing thought that this is more than just another move to a new house. I am doing the job that someone else would have been tasked to do at some point without me, painfully sorting through these pieces of fabric.

Try as I might to push these thoughts away, my tired body won't allow it tonight. It wants to feel sad, leaking eyes and all. I suppose that is just the way it will have to be.

It seems like such a ridiculous thing to consider this gluttony of goods a problem, or give them any meaning at all. But I keep stumbling across long-forgotten items...my (grand)Papa's crucifix that was passed on to me when he died years ago, pictures of my nephews when they were babies, ticket stubs from concerts I barely remember attending, cards full of goodbye messages from former colleagues. They stop me in my tracks—force me to pause mid-motion and consider where I've been, what I can't bear to part with, what I will leave behind when I go.

$69.7 Billion Worth of Misery

The National Eating Disorders Collaboration in Australia has produced an info-graphic that shows the estimated total social and economic cost of eating disorders in that country to be $69.7 billion Australian dollars in 2012.

I can't speak to the accuracy of this figure or how it was determined, but suffice it to say there's a whole lotta misery going on. Let's consider that price tag for a moment. That is more than four times the value of the total B.C. health budget.

I have tried not to harp on the issue of eating disorders—dwelling instead on my failing kidneys—and that should be an indication of the shame associated with this topic for me. But lately, I have been thinking that I would be abundantly annoyed if my passing is described on some official document as the product of a faulty organ. I am telling you here and now, that will by no measure be the cause.

I suspect it won't make any difference, and I won't be around to argue about it, but it is suddenly important to me that the facts are straight. I won't get into the details of where I am with my disorder—I know that talk of numbers and specifics can be incredibly triggering to someone who is suffering—but I will say that even the prospect of death hasn't warmed its icy grip.

Rock bottom after rock bottom, and still it goes on.

But, despite the uncomfortably personal nature of what I have shared, this is not about me. It is about the possibility of shaking some anonymous someone who has a son or daughter, friend or acquaintance, in danger of falling down this rabbit hole. You may not be able to stop them, but maybe you can cushion their fall.

I know that people in all sorts of desperate circumstances find hope, even in situations far more despairing than my own, and I really do want the glass to be half full. But I am trying so hard to speak the truth—to call a spade a spade as if it really matters.

This is one of those times when this blog is equivalent to a confessional, and my penance is facing the risk of being written off as just another nutty nobody who lacked gumption. So that is where I sit, trying to convey just how real the consequences of this disorder can be. And the dollar value of this lost cause? Priceless...

· · · · · · · · · ·

MONDAY, OCTOBER 14
Seeing the Finish Line

All the items on the list have been dutifully crossed off, one by painful one, and now just the last-minute touches remain before we call this house done and the sale sign erected. Every single member of my family is wasted by the effort, particularly my dad and mom. It is hard for me to witness how very much they want to take this burden off me, the stress and all of the tasks that I don't have the energy for. They are not young, and it seems so wrong, so twisted around, to be this helpless.

I can't say thank you often enough—can't begin to express what it means to me. At the same time I can't bear watching everyone around me—my sister, her husband—well past exhaustion performing the tasks that I couldn't finish, or couldn't even begin.

Don't get me wrong—I did a lot of work myself before I hit a wall and my body said "enough." It hits me over and over again with a rock-hard slap what this really means. My sense of urgency, my desperation to have this finished, stems from a desire to spare Kirk the monumental task of figuring this out on his own. That may sound condescending—a suggestion that he would be incapable of sorting it—which is obviously far from the truth. He has worked incredibly hard, probably harder than anyone, at this process. But I guess I know him well enough to know that he would be too proud to ask for the things I have at least been able to contribute to, things that I know my family would willingly do without hesitation if he were able to bring himself to call on them.

But we don't have time to waste. We are getting it done together and we all understand why it is necessary, why now is the time. It is a surrender—a waving white flag to what we have accepted; what we know will come. We all see the finish line clearly. We just don't know when it will be crossed.

. . . .

WEDNESDAY, OCTOBER 16
Shelter

If you stand in a particular spot on our front porch and strain your eyes to peer through the trees, you can see just a sliver of the Pacific Ocean.

This is the closest to that body of water that I am likely to get, from a home-ownership perspective. The bonus of living here is that less than a block away from home, I can stand and gaze at it to my heart's content, or climb down onto the rocks on the beach and write, hidden from the tourists who pass by. The sad truth is, since we moved here, I have in no way taken advantage of this proximity. I have taken it for granted in its familiarity, sniffed at its beauty as if it were nothing special. I should have stopped to breathe it in and appreciate it more often. With the prospect of moving house on the horizon, I know that this ocean will never again be quite as close to home as it is now. It won't be too far away—still near enough to feel the power of its breezes, the sweep of seagulls passing by—but no longer close enough to touch.

There is something about preparing a house for sale that makes you fall in love with it again. It's the ironic side-effect of addressing all the things you couldn't bring yourself to do to improve your own living space, but will willingly do for a complete stranger. As though a restart button has been pressed, every angle of my view has changed. It has made me nostalgic about our wee magnolia tree in the front yard, which began its life so tenuously when we moved in and now erupts in the most brilliant and delicate white flowers in the spring; the wisteria that has been coaxed into a lush wig for the pergola in our driveway; and the view through our front window of the foliage of the old trees that line the adjacent street.

This is the stature of a real house; not a box in the sky smashed up against, above or below someone else's life. I never hoped to dream I would have something so beautiful. And while I know a house does not make a home, this is where my heart is.

I'm trying very hard to make myself believe that I am ready to accept a paler version of this home and all its beauty, which some-how I couldn't really see until now.

· · · · · · · · · ·

SATURDAY, OCTOBER 26
Facing Facts

It takes a whole lot of time for things to sink in, for the truth to seep into the brain and, once it is firmly lodged there, to face it. This is where I am now, ready to fill out endless forms, finally sub-mitting to all of the necessary steps that must be taken to sort out how I will carry on financially until the end. There are pages and pages of them. I dutifully check off the boxes one by one.

I lived for many years with the luxury of a good job with all of the trappings of security that trail in its wake, but I have always looked at those in more precarious situations and thought, "There but for the grace of God go I." I was always terrified that the security blanket might be torn away and I would find myself back where I was when I was just starting out, when everyday living felt like I was walking around with a begging bowl.

That unrelenting fear of want, the fierce pride that makes any whisper of dependency unbearable, will be lost on people whose parents, unlike mine, did not grow up in the long shadows of the Great Depression.

By now, my grand schemes to crawl back into the world of work—even temporarily—have been all but extinguished. I have formally dissolved the wee consulting firm I half-heartedly launched last year, putting an end to my weak attempt at self-employment.

My anxiety about this is so great that I find myself trying to calculate the financial advantage of not being here at all. It has come down to that—a weighing up of my liability, the cost of prolonging this slow decline.

With all of this worry and the stress of the impending move, I have literally made myself sick. I curl into a feverish ball only to emerge momentarily for the endless cleaning required when showing your sanctuary to potential buyers.

. . . .

THURSDAY, OCTOBER 31
Weighing Things

I want to preface this entry by warning that it contains numbers. As much as I want to avoid them, it is not something I can do right now, so I am giving those with an active eating disorder the gentle advice not to trigger yourself by reading any further.

If you don't fall in that category, you might not truly understand how numbers work on the disordered brain. They read like challenges, or some kind of heavenly ordained permission to drop down to a lower weight than whatever plateau you may be hovering on.

When I went to see my doctor yesterday and stepped onto her scale, she informed me that I was almost 10 pounds smaller than on my last visit. That leaves me at the approximate body weight I was at when I was 10 years old.

It is a significant change, even for me, in a relatively short time. It helps explain why sitting and lying down are becoming increasingly uncomfortable. I have lost so much of my natural cushioning that even the sofa feels like a series of sharp angles.

We are past the point, my doctor and I, where such news is treated with shock or urgency, as it might have been years ago. In the past, an in-patient stint or other intervention option might have been raised. But by now she knows me so well; what I am and am not capable of doing in response to this. And, frankly, she knows it wouldn't make things better. Over the years she has seen enough patients who, like me, are no longer teenagers by a long shot. Her biggest fear is how this weight loss might destabilize my kidneys, so she asked me to step up my visits for a while.

I wonder whether the monumental stress and physically demanding work of preparing our house for sale has played a role in this drop in weight. Unlike many other times in my life, I can't say I was actively trying to land here. Or perhaps this is just a byproduct of my failing kidneys—toxins that are no longer filtered out of my blood now just sit in my system, making the prospect of eating very unappealing at times.

In any event, my brain knows I am at a dangerous point. I know that this could bring an end to the relative stability of the very limited kidney functioning I have left.

My doctor gently asked whether subconsciously I was trying to hurry this along, and that question sits with me now like a lump in my throat that I cannot swallow.

Do I just want this to be over?

Is my mind, as it feeds on itself, capable of finding a reason to try to extend my time—my voice—perhaps out of love for the people who are closest to me? Or am I trying to spare them and myself any more of this?

For today I am counting my blessings—one by one by one—and reminding myself that there must be some reason my body has hung in this long despite such neglectful tending.

November
2013

SUNDAY, NOVEMBER 3
Labels

I am a hybrid, formally diagnosed with two of the many permutations of eating disorders. For many sufferers of bulimia, outward appearances can be deceiving—dangerously so. Many maintain a weight at or even above an ideal body mass index. This means that on any given day you could walk right past someone who is suffering, overtaken by their internal demons, and have no clue.

We understand—or think we do—the physical indications that a person is living with anorexia, but even then you would be mistaken in thinking that its sufferers are wholly a parade of skeletons. And you would not be alone, upon seeing a televised interview of a sufferer, in thinking to yourself, "but she/he doesn't look *that* thin." Even I must admit my guilt in this area.

I have the symptoms, traits and behaviours of both anorexia and bulimia, and my weight over the long years has fluctuated wildly along the way. My point is that appearances and labels are deceiving, and can't be taken as an accurate barometer of a person's well-being.

Sadly, a byproduct of my own disclosure is that I have been confronted by the reality of just how many of the men and women

I know carry some form of negative body image or food issues around with them like a loaded knapsack every day.

It is pervasive, debilitating, a landslide of judgment and self-hate. An eating disorder? Maybe not...but disordered eating? Very much so.

Many groups and organizations are actively trying to change the dialogue—to preach body love and self-acceptance—but most people understand what a mountain of deeply ingrained cultural resistance stands in the way. The labels are just another way of dismissing people, denying their unique story and dignity and casting them off as some kind of wholesale imperfection.

We are all so much more complex than a textbook description, so much more than any of our flaws or shortcomings. Yet we give ourselves permission to attach all sorts of bias to our thinking around anyone struggling with mental health and addiction, blaming and shaming them in a way we would never dare do to a patient suffering from, say, cancer.

The commentary in our society disturbingly reflects this on a daily basis, as does the fact that we blatantly drop these issues to the bottom of the priority list in favour of emergency fixes.

It is time to acknowledge the pervasiveness of this insidious problem, get over our preconceived notions and face facts. We are here, and you can't afford to wait until our funerals to acknowledge that we deserve so much more.

. . . .

SUNDAY, NOVEMBER 3

Just in Case

Sometimes I think about how I would end this—what my key message would be, as it were (that's the communications professional in me talking). It is certainly not to hold myself up as an example, nor to lay blame for my illness at anyone's feet (except perhaps at my own), nor to tell you that even things that are deeply, irreparably flawed can be beautiful—because there is nothing beautiful about this.

I guess what I have learned, over and over, is how sharing this has somehow shaken certain truths to the surface and blown away my natural instinct not to be overly familiar or affectionate. Sharing my story has brought connections into my life that I would never have experienced had these feelings and experiences remained stored in my head, and has inspired so many people to offer me—without a hint of demand for reciprocation—the most overwhelming love. I wish I could have learned to embrace such affection many years ago.

Even still, I'm inclined not to dismiss but perhaps temper some of this emotion. Human instinct must prevent us from being completely honest when someone is dying. Hidden behind many of the good wishes in these same people are the scars of past incidents—times when I have hurt others with my words through impatience or thoughtlessness. And those are the moments I can't let go of, the moments I torture myself with. I am so deeply and irrevocably shaken by the hurtful things I have done and said in my life that I cannot take back—that none of us can ever take back—things that even a long line of sorries can't erase.

So I suppose what I am left with is that it has been so worthwhile to expose these truths—that it is worth giving someone the words you might share if you thought they were in trouble. And, to the extent that you can, it helps to keep your list of sorries much shorter than mine.

The Matter of Time

Sometimes a person just *knows*. Information passes by osmosis into the bloodstream, winding its way to the brain, where it breeds a quiet awareness that change is occurring. I guess this explains some of my recent posts.

A visit to my lovely specialist yesterday only confirmed what my heart and my head already knew, which is that the lab numbers I have been trying so hard to have faith in are no longer reliable where my kidneys and I are concerned. Under this system, the calculations of the level of toxins in my blood are based on an "average man," a profile that clearly doesn't match me, given my current size. This, combined with the marked escalation in my symptoms (the scientific term is "the feeling crappy factor"), points to a sharp downturn in my prognosis. My specialist explained that, in his experience, once the symptoms are felt, it is not a slow decline. The cheery prospect of having a possible five more years ahead of me has dwindled to "maybe" seeing 2014 through.

It was not a tremendous surprise to hear him say it. My body has sent this message to me loud and clear for weeks now. And yet... well, let's just say that my drive home from his office felt very, very long.

If past experience is anything to go on, the full weight of this information will roll over me later, when I least expect it.

I have spent so much of my energy trying to make Kirk and myself ready for this moment emotionally, financially and legally. Now I am hit in the face by it, not by the theory of it, but by the reality of it, marching relentlessly toward me, the pace ever increasing—it will not stop. I have acted on this information with a sense of urgency, and now I see that it was not misplaced.

Right now I just feel numbed by it, as though if I feed the dogs and clean the counters and write these words, it will go away. Yet I hear its approach, feel it when I breathe, see it when I am brave enough to look into my own eyes. It is coming...it is coming...it is here.

. . . .

I'm less than nothing
Can no longer rise to the occasion
Now every challenge
Defeats me.
You've stripped away my confidence
All of you
And remind me every day
I don't live up to my previous billing
My energy's been stripped away
How alone can you be
How long can you let your dreams slip by you
Without even the will to fight
To claim your life
As your own
How long can you be empty

. . . .

TUESDAY, NOVEMBER 5

Visiting Hours

There is something that has been weighing on me lately—an issue I continue to contend with that unsettles me, makes me feel guilty and anxious in equal measure. You see, my writing about this—the ticking clock that I can hear counting down my days—has prompted many people to lovingly say they would like to see me, spend time with me—pop by for a visit, or maybe coffee or lunch. (And when I say "many" please know that it is not a stampede—I am not Beyoncé and only attract so many followers!)

I have said no—in the gentlest way I know how—more times than I can say. First, I must clarify that I never was and never will be a social butterfly. My workday life—when it existed—just didn't include the regular round of coffee dates and lunches with friends that many people seem to enjoy. It is not that these things never occurred, just that on a normal day I just didn't leave the office for anything but short bursts. I suppose I could have done, but frankly, it just wasn't my cup of tea—or coffee, if you will.

So now, after more than a year away from work and eight months since I found out my kidneys were failing, the requests to get together have escalated. While I understand it is not all about me—people are genuine in their desire to see me or give me a hug—the prospect fills me with a severe anxiety that I cannot get past.

I've reached a point at which I am so self-conscious about the way I am, the way I look, that I have to avert my eyes from neighbouring cars at stoplights to avoid being seen. I keep asking Kirk if he can see what I see . . . if what my eyes are telling me is true. I see recent pictures of myself and have to look away. I can't stand it—it makes me cry out loud.

I don't want to be remembered this way. I can't pretend that I can give people all of the energy I normally would to reassure them, to comfort them, to explain. I say all this as a sincere effort to explain why I have said no, and as an apology. It is not because I don't love you or wouldn't want to hug you back. It is not that I don't appreciate your generosity and kindness. It is just that, for right now anyway, the contact is more than I can endure.

For What I Have Done, For What I Have Failed to Do

When it comes to religion, I suppose I would fall into the "lapsed Catholic" camp.

When I was young and church was a regular part of my life, I learned a prayer in which you beseech the Virgin Mary "and all of the angels and saints" to forgive you. "In my thoughts and in my words, for what I have done, for what I have failed to do..."

I have always been a word person so when I hear a good line, it tends to stick with me. Setting aside the religious aspect for a moment, it is the words themselves that I find beautiful, and over the years I have found myself returning to them. They are a part of who I am. At times, more specifically at *this* time, I go back to them a lot, roll them around on my tongue and try to absorb their power. This is a time to be grateful for what I have had—but also a time of atonement, of reckoning, to reflect on certain moments, and to do what I can to let them go.

I am always suspicious of anyone who says they have no regrets, as it implies to me that the one million errors, omissions and deliberate transgressions we inflict upon each other in the course of our daily lives are OK as long as we have learned something from them. My life has been a constant reliving of these moments. They are familiar ghosts who fly back into my mind just when things are getting good, to remind me I am not worthy or, at a minimum, did not try hard enough. That is the place guilt brings you to—and when you live there, it is hard to move on.

I have said before that from where I sit, the only things that really need to be said are, "I love you" and "I am sorry," and there are only so many ways to convey these things in a manner that is meaningful and real. I say them a lot to the people closest to me; try always to remember to say something before I hang up the phone. I suppose the phrase "it goes without saying" may apply here, and yet I keep yammering on, trying to perfect the message; trying to genuinely say to people I have hurt that I am sorry—and trying to be OK with the fact that for some people, that may not be enough. The expectation of forgiveness is not a given—this I have learned. There are some situations where it may never be earned. These things must be confined to the "unresolved" box and the lid shut tight. Not forgotten, but left to rest without my constant fussing, my meaningless interventions, my overpowering need to be absolved.

. . . .

WEDNESDAY, NOVEMBER 6

Where Is My Mind

It was Kirk's son Aaron who introduced me to the Pixies' song that inspired this post. In earlier years, a visit with him always meant taking home with me a new band or song that immediately became one of my favourites.

I thought of the title of this song because one of the symptoms that has started to creep in—and perhaps has been active in me for a much longer time than I realize—is a certain confusion and lack of focus that comes from starving your body and brain of the fuel it needs to stay sharp. This is compounded by my failing kidneys; as the body stops eliminating certain toxins, reactions can become irrational and difficult to control. Unfortunately, it is the people closest to me who bear the brunt of this—and I wish I could say it wasn't happening, but it is.

I was never beautiful—never the pretty girl—but I always seemed to have two small things going for me: my sense of humour, and a certain sharpness that at least I could try to hold up in my favour. The prospect of losing clarity, my ability to be articulate, my control over what I am feeling or saying, terrifies me more than anything else. This is why writing—this attempt to focus—has become more than a pastime for me. I find myself going over and over the words, looking for mistakes, for words that I missed, for thoughts that don't come out right.

Then I worry that I won't even have the clarity to recognize the problem as it gets worse, and that people around me will be too polite to point it out. In some ways it is why I feel I have to get it all out now, before I decline even further. I just pray I will have the good sense left to know when to stop—to walk away and keep what is left of my thoughts to myself.

. . . .

THURSDAY, NOVEMBER 7
Riding the Roller-Coaster

It is a fact, in this new orbit in which we spin, that Kirk and I are on very different rides. Selling and buying a home is stressful and emotionally draining at the best of times, but for obvious reasons, this time that stress has an added girth to it. Naturally, we aren't feeling the same enthusiasm we did when we were moving up the property ladder, rather than down it. In addition, we are simultaneously juggling one million different decisions and tasks, trying to wrap up other unfinished business in our lives. All of it is difficult to face; a reminder of my mortality.

We struggle with our words, taking pains not to blame one another when it becomes clear that we are not coming at this from the same place. The past week has been full of new information and big strides, with meetings and appointments that have brought everything into sharper focus and made the way forward much clearer. To me, this feels like ticking boxes and taking care of business, small victories that put my racing mind at ease.

Kirk experiences it very differently. All this "progress" does not inspire the same peace or excitement in him; just a sort of resignation, a deep sadness for what it all represents. It is the proverbial elephant in the room. In every potential property that we view together, we know that what we are seeing is a space that he will ultimately occupy alone. I talk about it with a sort of matter-of-fact practicality that seems perfectly reasonable to me, but it inspires little comment from Kirk. He is going along with it, but his heart is elsewhere.

I understand why it has to be this way. I want this to be wrapped up nicely and he is still looking at what is inside the box and mourning it. I can't bring myself to feel the sorrow of it all because if I did, I wouldn't be able to pick myself up off the floor long enough to make myself do the things I still need to do in order to get everything settled. I want to take care of some of the big decisions that Kirk might otherwise face alone, help him over some of the inevitable hurdles. But my drive—in my usual steam-roller style—to make it all happen yesterday is pushing Kirk in a way that sometimes feels cruel. He comes home from work each day to an avalanche of developments that I can't seem to spare him from.

He is one in a million. The fact that he has been as patient as he has—continued to go to work each day as if a landslide is not bearing down on us—fills me with an appreciation for him that I struggle to articulate. He simply doesn't want my absence to be hurried along. And that is the one thing I cannot spare him.

To Those Who Just Don't Get It

A dear person in my life sent me an LA *Times* op-ed yesterday explaining how not to talk to someone who is ill. I wish it were not applicable, but sadly, the examples they gave held a certain resonance for me. This is not a universal complaint by any stretch—there are many people in my life who have somehow known exactly what to say. But not everyone intuitively has this skill. Our denial about death and dying runs so deep, it's no wonder some people struggle to handle these conversations sensitively.

The fact is, I am dying, *ergo* I do not feel particularly well. There are still things I am quite capable of doing, but conserving my energy is important as I work to get my affairs in order. And although I love hearing from people, keeping up with them just takes more out of me than I can give some days.

Saying no has always been a difficult thing for me, so when I receive a curt response in return, I find it incredibly upsetting. Sometimes I find myself listening to people as they unburden themselves about how badly my situation is affecting them, rather than the other way around. Wishing it were happening to you rather than me is not particularly helpful, either. Really, where do I begin to respond to something like that?

The essential message in this article was that friends and supporters should try to direct that kind of commentary elsewhere, not to the person who is staring death in the face. You have the right to feel sad, to be angry, to feel helpless and overwhelmed, but it is best you pick someone other than the sufferer onto whom to unload these feelings.

The fact is, I am here, it is real and it is challenging enough to face what I need to do without adding other pressures that I have no space for right now.

. . . .

The 'To-Do' List

It is a surreal experience to take inventory of my thoughts these days. My mind is occupied by such diverse concerns as the merits of hospice care, the question of whether or not I might consider a feeding tube down the line (no), and paint colours for our new/old house.

It is almost impossible to think about the tasks that lie before me and the timing of all of the details without getting tripped up by the biting question of my ability to complete them. What kind of shape will my body and mind be in in two months' time when this move is due to take place? I write out my lengthening list of things to do and arrange while looking skeptically at myself and wondering if I am really the right person for this job.

So far it has all fallen into place surprisingly quickly, but there are still miles to go. I know it can be done, with one foot gently placed in front of the other, each task followed by the next. But what no one in the world can possibly tell me is whether I will be here to see it all through.

. . . .

Deadlines

Any pending purchase of a strata unit brings with it the inevitable package of material for review. This weekend, I waded through pages of it: meeting minutes, bylaws and financial records. As would be expected with most any property, a few red flags popped up; things that will require some follow-up before we can decide whether or not to proceed with the purchase. It is a fact that within our new budget, property options—particularly those that will allow two dogs—are limited. So now begins a series of discussions that will make or break this deal.

I can't seem to reconcile the pressing urgency of our short time frame with my refusal to compromise on things. I am done in with the worry of it all and my body is not keeping up. I feel an over-whelming need to get this right, to get us settled into a sanctuary where Kirk and the dogs will be comfortable, healthy and happy. This is my last big job—the thing on which I have pinned all of my hopes—and in so many ways, I just can't afford to get it wrong. Home and everything it represents is all I can see right now. I know I have been rushing things, charging forward, because I am so very aware that time is speeding by me—I don't have the luxury of extending the search for perfection forever.

So much is weighing on me—what we are giving up, as well as what we will transition to; the fact we are in this position at all; the fact that we are facing this move while still absorbing the reality that I am every day inching closer to the end.

I am trying so hard to be excited about the new place. But for today, I am just wary of my choices and feeling incredibly tired.

. . . .

TUESDAY, NOVEMBER 12
Sold

As of 4:51 p.m. today, our house is sold. It came down to two almost identical offers—a young couple who had another property to sell and an older couple who didn't. The older couple won out. After all of the toil, the worry, the cleaning, the showings—it feels strangely anticlimactic. I look around me and somehow it already feels like it is slipping away. Maybe some part of me has already said goodbye to this house, while another wants to cling on tightly and not let go.

It is a beautiful house. I knew it was meant for us the moment I saw it on the realtor's website. It was not perfect, but the next best thing to it. It was in the right area, not too big and not too small, just right; a dream that did come true. This is the house where Kirk's first grandchild, Aanji, spent his first Christmas; where we said goodbye to our wee cat Chaos a few days after moving in; where we welcomed our ginger-eared Miss Daisy dog into our lives; where I made the decision to leave my job forever; where I got the phone call that told me my kidneys were failing. All of these things happened under this roof, and now we will walk away from it and into a future that is not certain. Our goal was to sell it quickly and with a minimum of fuss, and that we did. We did not linger. It was the right thing to do. And yet...

. . . .

WEDNESDAY, NOVEMBER 13
Oh Pandora, Shut Your Box

I write these posts in a vacuum of sorts. As I have done all my life, I spew out words when I have nowhere else to go. This is a place to vent where I am guaranteed not to get a piece of advice or a pep talk in return.

I write as if nobody but me is reading it. But one side-effect of putting it out there for the world to see is that the people I love feel hurt and helplessness when they open this Pandora's box of my thoughts. My situation is obviously not new information to them, but at times they seem to feel my words more deeply than at others—even Kirk, who resides at the same address. Late last night, his daughter Miranda called me from Toronto in tears to tell me she loved me, that she wished she could be here to help ease us through these next stages.

I know what I have shared in my writing is not a comfort. It remains difficult for certain people to read. But I have gone so far past the days of "How are you?" and "I am fine." I am belted into this journey—this telling of truths. I feel the twinge of their reactions, but not enough to take it back, because that is impossible for me now. It has to be done. Every painful word must be recorded—every fear, every thought, every joy, every apology—a commitment to myself that, for once, I am keeping. Not because it doesn't hurt, but because I don't know how to do this any other way. So to add to my list of sorries is a big one to those who have felt wounded in some way by these words. There is simply no Band-Aid big enough to cover my chattering heart.

. . . .

FRIDAY, NOVEMBER 15

We Could Be Hit By a Bus Tomorrow

Since I started watching my own personal countdown clock and musing on the question of how long I have left, my mom has been quick to interject that nobody knows the real answer to this question, and likes to remind me of the bus thing—not that I spend a lot of time walking in traffic lately. And it is true that not even my learned specialist nor my family doctor can give me a date with any particular accuracy. Everyone who goes through something like this is on their own unique journey.

My body will take its own sweet time with this. It sends me signals in the form of symptoms, like smoke rings circling in the sky, imparting information that is difficult to interpret and even harder to ignore. If I am outdoors and I find myself face to face with a crow in our yard, I'll wonder if it, like a vulture, is aware of my imminent demise. Is that why it is staring at me with such intensity?

For a controlling person like me, this lack of certainty is very hard to take—though even that is not nearly as frightening as the prospect of reaching a point when I may be totally dependent on other people to get around. Having some stranger involved in the little routines of life—that, more than anything else, is the thing I dread the most.

But only time will tell when or if that moment will come along—and for now, it's telling nothing.

. . . .

MONDAY, NOVEMBER 18

Legacies

When you are childless, the notion of leaving a legacy—someone who will carry a tiny piece of your spirit into the future—is a moot point. I used to wonder who would take care of me when I got old. Who would take any interest in how I was managing? Now this is an irrelevant concern—at this stage there is no prospect of reaching a "ripe old age."

In some respects, we get a preview of the feeling of losing someone when a beloved co-worker moves on to another position or city. In the beginning, their loss is deeply felt, their name frequently raised in discussion, their empty desk a reminder of their absence. But sooner or later it happens; that desk is occupied by a completely different person. The inside jokes are no longer shared.

The echo of their name grows dimmer, and while they may roll fleetingly across your mind in moments of nostalgia, those moments become less frequent. You may keep in touch faithfully at first, sharing news all of the goings-on, but that too will begin to fade as a natural letting-go takes over. As they say, no one is indispensable; we can all be replaced. At least, this is what we often repeat in the context of our working lives.

I don't know if this idea of leaving a legacy is even important—the prospect that a piece of me might live on in some way. And yet it is something one thinks about. Over time, everyone who knew me will move on. Time will do its work, and their memory of me will inevitably fade—which is as it should be. It is only natural, after all.

· · · · · · · · · ·

WEDNESDAY, NOVEMBER 20

Dying With Dignity?

The phrase "death with dignity" has over time become synonymous with the right-to-die movement, which promotes the view that individuals should have some say on how they exit their own life. This phrase has become an accepted part of the cultural lexicon, having been regurgitated so often that one doesn't question its meaning upon hearing it. But the more I think about it, I wonder if anybody really dies with dignity.

I can't quite reconcile that idea with the helplessness that I anticipate feeling when the end comes. Nothing about relinquishing my body into someone else's hands seems all that dignified to me. Quite the opposite, in fact.

I suppose every cause needs a good hook—something that makes the whole campaign sing. In this case the notion of "dignity" serves to elevate death above the negative and turn it into a positive.

It is not that I don't support an individual's right to choose—I do. But I also think that the pain of those choices—the messiness of the whole business—gets lost in the discussion somehow. I suspect that most people do not meet the end with their heads held high. To me, it seems the whole business is about abdicating your will, handing yourself over to others. One can only hope that the "others" won't hinder the process. Who trumps whom: the people providing care? The family? The patient? I hope I know the answer to that question.

....

SATURDAY, NOVEMBER 23

One Pill Makes You Larger and One Pill Makes You Small

Drug commercials have become the subject of many comic bits for good reason. After hinting a drug will change your life for the better, in gory detail they recite its horrendous side-effects. I don't ignore these warnings on the medications I now take on a daily basis, but frankly I have found that taking medication to relieve unpleasant symptoms is often a case of swapping one form of suffering for another.

I started a new medication today, and I have to say that I stopped in my tracks when, after swallowing the first pill, I noticed the cautionary notes. Among the helpful suggestions from the pharmacy was—and I am not making this up—"Call if you find you are doing things while you are asleep." Perhaps they should be more explicit here. Precisely what "things" are they referring to? Cooking a gourmet meal? Sending faxes? Light gardening? And how exactly am I supposed to know this if I am asleep at the time?

Clearly questions they didn't have time for in the "patient counselling messages."

My latest drug comes with the warning that it may make it difficult to absorb other medications, which is a bit of a problem under the circumstances. It doesn't much matter in the scheme of things. These are not cures, just an exercise in symptom management. Swallow, rinse, repeat every day, and hope the treatment isn't worse than the disease.

. . . .

SATURDAY, NOVEMBER 23
There Is No Free Pass

The thing you must come to grips with very quickly when you are dying is the fact that although your life is ending, that doesn't mean everyone else's is too. Events take place. Life happens. Milestones come and go, and plans are made for the future. Line-ups don't get shorter, bills still arrive, and no one gives you a pass that says because you don't feel particularly well, your clothes will hoist themselves into the washing machine. People still say and do stupid things, and you do too. You don't become automatically wiser, more sensitive, or more knowing.

Your sense of urgency is not necessarily shared by anyone else; your search for meaning is not necessarily relevant to anyone around you. You still stumble along, expecting everything and everyone to be different. But it isn't, and they aren't. They can't be. We aren't built that way—life doesn't move that way.

Even if you are not alone, in many ways you feel you are. You are the only one on this particular journey in your house, perhaps on your street.

You are not unique in your suffering—far from it. Other people have struggles too, and their journeys may be even more perilous than your own. But you can't fully absorb someone else's story because you have no capacity for it, and life won't stop long enough for you to make room to take it on. All you have is this long slow ride—the hours, the days, the ticking clock—on this part of the road that you walk alone, no sun glinting in your eyes, the crisp air all around you. The end will surely come whether you will it closer or dread its arrival.

This is how it has to be; movement all around you and the fear of standing still.

··········

Signs—Everywhere a Sign

The last few times I have spent time with my mom, she has started to cry upon seeing me. I confess these days I have a bit of a Nora Desmond-like look about me (the Carol Burnett version), but when my mere appearance inspires this kind of response, it raises feelings in me that are hard to put into words. I do not walk in her shoes so I have only an inkling of how hard this must be, not just because she knows I will not recover from this, but because she feels helpless to stop this train.

It might be different if this had come out of the blue, but she is shouldering the weight of many, many years of watching this unfold. Right from the moment of diagnosis, she has understood more than anyone else in my life that there was no fight left in me, knew as soon as I said the words "no intervention" why this seemed the logical—no, necessary—route to take. It is not for lack of love on her part, just a quiet resignation to the ways things have been and are now.

Ironically, she knows that I would fight and push hard to help anyone I loved who might land in trouble. I'd be opening up my wallet, intervening in any way I could, to try to fix the problem or make it go away. But in the context of my own life, there has grown an ever taller and thicker wall that seems to stand in the way of fighting for my own well-being. After a few decades, you stop even attempting to jump over it.

Every month I dutifully get my lab work done, and every month the numbers look more out of whack. Last week there was another reckoning, another series of numbers to contrast and compare. I really don't need to open up these reports at all. I see their results in my mother's eyes, in the way my nephew averted his gaze several times when we met the other day—not in a mean way, but just because he could read the information written all over my face.

We all see it. It is inescapable now. I am repeating myself—I know this. It is the same story repackaged, the same lyrics; repeat, repeat, repeat. I think I want it to stop, but then again, I don't.

I wondered, as I looked around the rooms on our final walk-through, whether the townhouse we are buying will actually be a place I will ever move in to. Wonder, if I am "lucky," as my doctors tell me, to die this way, what the "un-lucky" people must feel like. Wonder how—and how soon—it will stop. Questions are followed by more questions, and at the moment, I have nothing but time for them to fester and multiply.

The fact is, I don't feel well. My most recent prescription caused a horrible reaction (which serves me right for mocking the topic earlier) and the "comfort measures" I signed up for seem out of reach. I can talk to my doctor and try again—try something else—try to stop feeling bad about feeling bad, and get on with it.

If this journey were a book, I'd have turned the corner of this page over carefully and put it back on the shelf. Enough.

. . . .

WEDNESDAY, NOVEMBER 27
You Can't Always Get What You Want

There was an article in the *New York Times* the other day entitled "How Doctors Die." The premise of the piece was basically that doctors are one-up on the rest of us because they have the advantage of knowing precisely what to ask for to stay reasonably pain-free and comfortable on their journey to the light.

I am sure this is not representative of every physician's journey and some must be just as deeply in denial about the whole thing as the rest of us. But it would be an undeniable advantage to be able to identify what you need as you wander down the unfamiliar path toward death.

It is a bit embarrassing for someone who tends to know, generally speaking, what is going on, to find oneself floundering. At any given moment, I find myself struggling to determine whether what I am feeling represents the beginning of the end, or whether in fact I passed that point weeks or months ago. And if I start feeling worse, I can't decide whether I need to call in reinforcements or just wait for it to pass.

Had I chosen dialysis, the nature of that treatment would require more regular check-ins and monitoring by health professionals who presumably could help identify some of these things. But as it is, in between visits with my doctor or specialist I am basically left to try to figure it out myself. To be honest, I am a very poor judge and my tolerance level for soldiering on is pretty high after all of these years. I started from a place where not feeling optimal was my normal. I know enough to say when I am far beyond that point, but how far exactly?

Some days it is just so hard to distinguish what you want from what you need; to be able to say where it hurts and know who and when to ask for help. There is no road map for this—it just takes you toward a place you do not know anything about, with no idea when you will reach your destination.

No two people's trips are exactly the same, so while you can read about the signs, they may not necessarily apply, or come in the order you were expecting. For someone who has always strived for control—largely in vain, given the randomness of life—this is beyond me.

Knowing what you are capable of giving and what you need to receive may seem straightforward enough, but sometimes even these questions are impossible to answer.

· · · · · · · · · ·

SATURDAY, NOVEMBER 30
This is the Sound of One Voice

It is official now, and witnessed, legally binding: my advance care directive, which states what I will and will not consent to in terms of medical intervention at the end. Clear-eyed and—eventually—level-headed, I completed it with my doctor, and with my sister and Kirk by my side. All the documents have been copied in triplicate and dutifully shared. Another piece of this puzzle set gingerly in place.

We discussed and considered the next steps together. We agree that things are moving much faster than we expected. Home nurse visits are likely soon; a step that on the one hand feels like submission, and on the other seems a welcome reprieve. Maybe they'll only be necessary for a short time, until this particular phase passes. Or maybe not.

We have shifted from the prospect of five years to a year, and now, possibly, to weeks. The fact is, nobody really knows. These discussions are surreal. So many papers to sign and things to be said. My eyes were closing on the car ride home. These windows get shorter—as does, thankfully, the list of things to be done.

Bravery flew out the window long ago. I flip from resignation—a forced dismissal of emotional response so that I can focus instead on what needs to be done—to overwhelming fear of the things I cannot orchestrate.

I have shared more than I ever intended in these pages—more than was necessary—but still not everything. Our wounds are as deep as our secrets, and there are some things better left unsaid. To be honest, on many days I don't know why I started writing this, but now that it is out there, I suppose I am released, in part, from the experiences I related here.

As I have said before, everything that has happened happened for a reason. I made decisions that are mine alone, and the consequences are what I invited, what I allowed. Even when I picked the wrong path, I can be thankful that I had choices; that I had the means, the support and physical capacity to choose.

Writing this blog has been my release, a place to go when my thoughts just couldn't stay locked inside me any longer. Even now, I feel a desperate need to explain myself, to even the scorecard, even with people who have no regard for me and maybe never did. I feel compelled to try to win them over when the prospects of that are futile. I am frantic to make things OK.

I have been the beneficiary of more love and support than I ever deserved. The kindness of strangers. The forgiveness and understanding of those who knew me better, who saw my deeply flawed shell and loved me anyway.

How can I ever truly capture my gratitude for that?

And I will say again: if I let you down on any occasion, hurt you or disappointed you, please know from my heart I am so very sorry. No life is worth living if you cannot say that out loud and truly mean it.

December
2013

All That I Can Find to Give

I was fortunate in my working life to come across many dynamic and inspiring people, and while I hope I took the time to convey what they meant to me along the way, I now feel compelled to talk about one person in particular: the illustrious *Vancouver Sun* health reporter Pamela Fayerman. She is one of the few dedicated health-care reporters left in the newspaper business and her experience and knowledge shine through in the depth of her stories, in the questions she is compelled to ask.

Since I left my post, and in the months since my diagnosis, she has reached out to me repeatedly to see how I was doing, offering the resource of her considerable professional connections if necessary and generally demonstrating the depth of her caring.

Recently she challenged me on the topic of my eating disorder and asked whether there was anything I might have to offer after my decades-long battle that might be helpful or instructive to others who are suffering.

I have never seen my experience as much more than a cautionary tale that one cannot abuse one's body to the degree I have done without some form of reckoning.

In all honesty, the fact it took this long for me to experience a consequence as significant as kidney failure is a miracle. Many people—men and women—will die as a direct or indirect consequence of disordered eating, and it will often catch up with them much more quickly than it did in my personal experience. Of course, the physical toll is only one aspect to all of this. The emotional toll, not just for those who suffer but also for those who love them, is immeasurable.

The fact is, I read many times about the risks involved, and none of it could compel me to stop. I do not believe you can scare someone into changing their behaviour.

Back when I was young, before this behaviour had become so entrenched, the options for people like me were limited and, dare I say, primitive. I still do not believe that waiting until people are acutely sick, then throwing them into hospital for "stabilization" when they are emotionally ill-prepared for the consequences, is an effective or reasonable approach. Nor is it fair or sustainable to send a select few sufferers for extended stays in hospitals south of the border at a cost of millions of dollars. (It happens.)

I know that efforts have been underway in our own province to transform the approach to treatment as part of the broader mental health plan. The road back to health—for those who recover—is rarely a straight line. Some, like me, will not make it, while others will try literally dozens of times to recover before they are successful.

I feel that I am a poor candidate to give any advice on this topic, but I can offer the following:

1. Teach your children that "you've lost weight" is not a compliment they should strive for above all else.

2. If someone you love is suffering, understand that it is not about food and weight. It is about something so much deeper: fundamentally feeling unworthy. Unworthy of self-care, unworthy of love.

3. Know that you cannot force someone—as much as you would love to—to be well. You can be supportive and loving, but in the end and even with the best professional supports, they will need their own light and strength in order to overcome it.

4. If you struggle with your own issues with food and body image, seek help for that—to the extent you can—before visiting these issues on your children.

5. Recognize that eating disorders are not diseases of vanity, nor do you have to be a walking skeleton to suffer acutely from these conditions.

6. Do all you can in the early stages to facilitate the sufferer in accessing resources, whether that comes in the form of a trusted and knowledgeable family doctor, counsellor or other more targeted professional programs. As with any addictive behaviour, the more entrenched it is, the harder it is to prevail against it.

7. If you are a loved one or a support person, remember and acknowledge your own need for a helping hand, and don't be afraid to reach out. You will lead by the example of your own willingness to acknowledge that there is no prize for suffering alone.

8. Read everything and learn as much as you can about what type of supports exist in the community, and offer your support to those who are advocating to better address the overwhelming needs in this area.

Again, I am not a poster child for this condition, nor do I profess to have any particular answers. All I have are my thoughts, now facing the prospect of my own mortality after these decades.

If you are struggling, I send you all of the light and hope I have to give. You are worthy of love. You are worthy of leading a full and meaningful life.

··········

SUNDAY, DECEMBER 8

The Futility of Second Thoughts

As of tomorrow, I start receiving more rigorous medical support from a home care nurse, who will help address some of the symptoms that have kept me in physical discomfort for awhile now. Frankly, I waited too long to ask for it, but now it is on its way, to be administered by an angel of mercy, courtesy of our fine public health-care system.

The hard things I am about to share are wrapped in the warm prospect of this imminent support, along with the love, notes of comfort and prayers from special people in my life. All of that should not be lost in what follows.

I have recently been seriously thinking I should stop writing about this. In part, this is because I have been physically feeling quite wretched, and in part because I want so desperately to be one of those transcendent people whom others might admire for being plucky and positive and transformed at the end, and that is just not where I am.

I watched part of a CBC documentary series on end-of-life issues the other day, in which people with terminal illnesses and severe disabilities were arguing for and against assisted suicide. The story of one man in particular stood out. He was wheelchair-bound, with enough medical challenges to fill a dictionary—he had cerebral palsy and had had his colon and one of his kidneys removed. He passionately stated that despite his constant pain, he felt that life was precious and he feared that opening the door to a physician-assisted option might lead to people like him being seen as disposable.

More than once on this journey I have questioned my own motivation in choosing not to pursue dialysis or transplant, and have wondered whether certain people would regard this choice as a form of suicide, albeit a more complicated one—as an admission that I see my own life as disposable.

I will admit to you now that the worse my symptoms become, the more I have second-guessed this decision. Honestly, I have had moments when I imagine calling up the specialist and begging him to do everything and anything to make it stop, even after having explicitly written "no dialysis under any circumstances" in my advance care directive. But questioning my decision-making is familiar territory—and it doesn't take me long to return to my original stance because the reality of my bigger issues comes home to roost.

I call it a choice, but really, that is not fully accurate.

The wait list for kidney transplants is higher than for any other organ, filled with desperate people who either can no longer tolerate dialysis or medically have outgrown its usefulness. My specialist has already told me that I would not be a viable candidate for the transplant list unless I demonstrated a glimmer that I was prepared to overcome my eating disorder. Accepting dialysis would mean complying with a strict diet and controlling fluid intake, and this is not something my eating disorder could or would allow.

The fact is, I have descended below my fictional goal weight several times over. Now, even the prospect of imminent death doesn't stop me from stepping on the scale at least four times a day, scrutinizing it for a change in the position of the needle, calculating whether there might be time in the day to get it back to a point that is acceptable.

I still search the mirror for signs that my stomach is sticking out in a way that people who see me might label me "fat." And food now feels literally like poison. What cannot be filtered sits sickeningly in my system now, and that feeling stays with me most of the day.

If I truly believed I could manage my kidneys without having to contend with that other form of self-torture, I would not be in this place.

This is what it means to have given over your power to an eating disorder. The only respite from it is in irreversibly succumbing to it.

The second-guessing of my decision is also a fiction that denies the truth of what I have become. This is not easy or pleasant to admit, having walked the planet for most of my years trying to hide the obvious. And of all of the things that I was strong enough to accomplish, the one thing I couldn't—and still can't—accept is tipping the scale in the "wrong" direction. This single-minded, pathetic train of thought overrides every other feeling, and all of my self-will. The most troubling aspect of what is to become of me in the coming weeks or months is the prospect that I will be bloated with fluid my body cannot eliminate at the end.

I tell you these truths not to invoke disgust or, worse, in some ways, your pity. This is a slice of my story. Nothing more. It is instructive only as a window into what it means to live in the world of an eating disorder.

This is not all that I am. It is not representative of the facets of my character that still fight on. But it is part of what has defined me. It is what has set this ride in motion, and therefore the story is not complete without it.

Comfort and Joy

Between the bureaucracy around the process of dying, the periods of deep self-reflection, and the gripping fear of what it might look and feel like for me at the end, there are other moments that balance out the noise. An unexpected message from a former colleague or a friend; a moment of laughter with someone I love over something quite trivial; moments when messages from my body do not invade the space. Moments of gratitude, of affection. The sense of accomplishment that comes from putting pieces into place to make the way forward feel more settled. Random, funny moments from my past that come back to me. Added to that, I now have regular check-ins from a lovely home care nurse who is helping to ease the way.

No matter what has happened, my life has not been without moments of beauty; the joy of discovering kindred spirits in all sorts of places where they were least expected.

If all you have to know me by are the words in this blog, then I would forgive you for believing I lack any kind of hope. In truth, I have endless amounts of it for the people in my life who are struggling with their own difficulties; who have pulled their heads up in the face of fear. It happens all around me. I've seen the power of such a transformation, and whatever my shortcomings, I still have faith in the possibility to overcome adversity. This often-bleak description of my own path should not be mistaken for doubt in the human spirit, for an absence of light in this landscape... or even for the absence of a smile.

Ho Ho Ho

The holidays—so loaded with expectation, so fraught with demands. Idyllic visions are not always compatible with reality.

I loved Christmas when I was a kid, when there was still an air of magic around the presents wrapped beneath the tree. But over the years I confess I went off it. I just couldn't find the feeling. The whole season now seems more about some kind of desperate consumer frenzy that becomes more frenetic with each passing year.

While I love the notion of giving, even that has got a bit out of whack. It's not easy trying to express something that money can't buy with trinkets, a poor substitute for the feeling. Over the years our efforts have gotten smaller. A few missed holiday parties... the eventual vetoing of holiday cards. Presents, mostly a miss.

Of course this year, with our imminent move on the horizon, the prospect of bringing more stuff into our lives is not a welcome one. And where I am right now, on borrowed time, it is surreal to see the crowds of people with less than joyful faces circling for parking. They descend upon the shopping malls like soldiers desperately tracking their quarry; hunting the perfect gift that might inspire more than a polite smile rather than a look of disappointment. The barrage of hawkers on television urge us to buy more, more, more, pumping up a frenzy of debt that most of us can ill afford.

This year, I am not part of any of it, really, other than as an onlooker from the observation deck. No one in my family is readily making commitments. We just don't know what each day will bring. We can't anticipate what all of this will look like in a few weeks' time. I beg them, no things. I don't need things right now. Not just because every new possession becomes another item to wrap up in a moving box but because I am past wanting presents. My family have already given me every ounce of their generosity and energy helping us to get through the sale of this house and the finding and purchasing of a new one, dealing with endless appointments and paperwork—all of the support it has taken all of us to get through each day. Nothing they could give me—or I could possibly give in return—could compare to this greatest and most humbling gift.

I know that for some, particularly those with little ones, the magic remains alive. There is a contingent of people who always embrace the holidays with enthusiasm—the parties, the time with friends. I watch the passing antics on social media with affection. But I am also acutely aware that many people will face this season with one less beloved face around their dinner table. There are those who are struggling with illness or some other affliction themselves, who will struggle through the cheer. To those people, I wish you the gift of breathing through it, of taking the prospect of the New Year as a beacon for healing. A gift not wrapped up in paper but held inside your heart, where the magic of the season should shine.

. . . .

WEDNESDAY, DECEMBER 11
You've Got a Fast Car

I'm channelling Tracy Chapman tonight and celebrating the small things that keep me going. It really means something to me now—those rare days on which I get in my own little car and drive, although it's never far, and not for long.

Driving, for me, was always about independence—the freedom to leave. Most times now, people ferry me around, put cushions on the seats for me to sit on, deposit me at home when the task or appointment is done.

In my youth, my friend's mom used to take us in her old and temperamental vw van to the mall parking lot when the stores were closed and let us practise driving a standard. We'd circle the rows haltingly, mastering the turn signals, pulling into parking spots, backing up and starting again. We were not allowed to turn on the radio, even though it was rarely functional. We felt so grown up traversing that empty space, so entitled.

When I was 15, my sister Karen had had her driver's licence for about a year. She and I were granted permission to skip the ride to Christmas dinner at my aunt and uncle's place with my parents, so as to make our own grand entrance hours later via our little red truck.

It was freezing in Prince George, where we lived at the time. After some begging on my part, Karen agreed that it would be safe for me to start the truck and warm it up for the ride. I was enthusiastically up for the task. I turned the key and waited for the magic to happen. Regrettably, I missed the step where you make sure the vehicle is in neutral. The truck and I promptly careened into the frozen cement block fence in front of which it was parked. It shattered on impact and the front of the truck crumpled.

I was not hurt, although frankly, my terror at the thought of confessing what had happened would have eclipsed any physical symptoms anyway.

The world didn't end. The truck and the fence were eventually fixed.

I don't know why I thought of that moment this evening. It's a story that often comes up around the holiday season, a parable that speaks to my determination to master any available means of escape—and my refusal to admit that I wasn't ready to go.

Oh Mercy, Mercy Me

It is amazing how much one can appreciate small improvements. It's been just over a week since I started receiving visits from wonderful home care nurses from the local health authority's palliative care at home program. I'm also trying out some new medications, and the relief that they have brought from some of my more debilitating symptoms has allowed me some small bursts of activity that I just didn't have the heart for earlier—and which, frankly, I thought might have passed me by.

The connection between the physical and emotional is so powerful. I find that when I am able to be present and breathe deeply, even for small parts of the day, it makes me giddy with happiness.

Everything is in place for our move. It feels like I can actually get there now—like it is possible that I will experience the new place. How much time I will have there is not a question I need to waste time contemplating, but getting there is a powerful motivator. It pushes me forward, a momentum with its own breath, its own life.

Everything has fallen into place so readily that one feels an almost divine sort of power behind it. Yes, there were a few missteps but overall every element felt orchestrated, right down to the parking spot that appeared directly in front of the door of the lawyer's office when we went in to sign the final papers on a busy Friday afternoon.

Everything is a sign—a portent of a light shining all around this process, as though it is understood that anything else might be more than we can take. And so this is just the way we need it to be—the way it should be now. I embrace it, feel myself moving into yet another stage. It feels more like acceptance, more like I am ready, not fighting what is coming with the same amount of fear. I am able to feel the love that keeps coming toward me from near and far, telling me it is going to be OK. I am strong enough for this. I am still here.

. . . .

Old Dogs and New Tricks (No, This Isn't a Dog Story!)

Time is measured differently when the finite nature of life becomes a reality. One sees things in ways one may have not contemplated before. And what I see most powerfully right now is how the things we hold secret—from ourselves, from the people we love, from the larger community we work and interact with—drive a wedge between us and the world. It is a chasm that grows deeper and wider over time, which makes traversing it to reach some kind of intimate connection less and less likely, and sometimes impossible.

The things we can't bring ourselves to share entrench us in a kind of false reality. Isolation creeps around that place in your heart where secrets live until all that echoes in your head is your own disappointed voice.

As painful as it has been for me personally to release so many of these pieces into the universe, looking them square in the eye, facing all of my weaknesses and owning up to them has been the most transformative experience of my life. It gives me great comfort to know that people in my life are very clear about all of these aspects of my story, all of these choices I have made, and have not abandoned me for them; just held me closer and closer.

My mom once told me a story. While I am fuzzy on the details, the moral was that it is our failings—the elements of ourselves that we find hardest to look at—that are in some ways the most beautiful things about us. These are the things that build our character; our empathy and humanity. It is the imperfections that inspire the greatest love.

I see that now in a way I never really appreciated before; a lesson it is not too late to absorb, not too late to feel.

. . . .

TUESDAY, DECEMBER 24
The Camera Never Lies

I have never been a fan of "picture day." I am not the kind of person who was ever confident that the photos that came back would be acceptable to me or anyone else.

But sometimes, these days, I am tempted to take a picture of myself. And is it any wonder? There seem to be cameras built into almost every electronic device around us. (Can the toaster be far off?)

This is by no means about vanity. It's more about checking to confirm that I am still here; to look anxiously at the person who stares back to see what ravages are showing and to try to reassure myself it is not so bad.

I confess this because I have been trying, with my sister's help, to put together a project involving pictures—a kind of visual post-mortem of my life. I find that while I am able to look at images from when I was very small, there are other periods that I have a great deal of difficulty looking at. In some respects—as I tried to explain to my sister last night—there is a huge swath of my life before I met Kirk that I seem to have mentally written off. It's not that I don't retain the memories, but seeing myself in those years when my self-hate and eating disorder were at their worst, is painful to me, no matter how hard I try to let that go.

My sister tries to reassure me, as sisters do, that she sees something completely different. I try to have faith in her instincts, not trusting my own. But it hits me every time I look at that face, trying to be something it is not, trying to be what it never was.

I suppose that I should know by now—and as this blog has shown me—that blocking out the "bad" stuff never works. Facing it, quite literally, is a necessary part of the journey.

....

THURSDAY, DECEMBER 26
If You Could See Yourself as Others See You

The title of this post is inspired in part by an unexpected note, rich in its beauty, that I received tonight from an old friend. She was part of a small circle of friends and family with whom Kirk and I spent time in the early years of our relationship. She recently stumbled across my blog and learned, through what I have shared, the truth about these past months. Perhaps she was able to place our time together in broader context.

Her words, coming the day after Christmas, struck me deeply, taking me right back to those early times with Kirk. It was my first experience of actually moving in with someone. I was keenly aware at the time that the "me" that Kirk, his children and the broader community who loved him had welcomed into their lives was not real. They did not know the truth about me and my eating disorder.

At the time, I believed that had I been up front about it, I would have risked everything. It was something that I had tried valiantly to hide, and at which I succeeded, until at last I was confronted by the prospect of sharing the same living space with other people for an extended period.

So the person they thought they knew was someone else, someone they perceived very differently. This person, as described in her note, is hard for me to recognize, even though I understand that may be difficult to accept.

Her words also stirred up some of the feelings I expressed in my earlier post; my insecurity about the impact my illness has had on my physical appearance. This morning I saw the images my dad took of me with my sister's family on Christmas Day. Seeing them, I recalled how I had struggled to find clothes to wear. Under the fabric, I was so deeply conscious of the port in my chest, which allows me to administer my own medication. I asked Kirk again and again—likely until he was deeply irritated—if I looked OK; if it was OK for me to leave the house. So when I shared an image captured with my sister today, I did it almost waiting for someone to tell me it is time to stop.

I suppose all of this brings me back to the question of what we really see when we look into each other's eyes. When we share moments that reveal something deeper, do we perceive in each other what we fail to perceive in ourselves? What version of me do others really know?

. . . .

FRIDAY, DECEMBER 27

Let's Have a Party!

After adamantly declaring that when I go meekly into the light, there will be no ceremony of any sort—a position I have stood firm on for months now—I appear to have turned a corner on that front. Having ruled out burial at sea, a funeral pyre lit by someone who dislikes me (a parting gift to them), and my standard position that my ashes should be stored in a closet out of people's way, I have landed on the idea of a good old "celebration of life" ceremony.

I have shifted to event-planning mode, considering the optimal timing and venue, anticipating the boredom factor at such events and thinking about how to pace things in such a way that we don't lose the audience.

I will admit this is a morbid pursuit, but some people have told me that something like this could be expected. Fair enough, I say, but let's try to keep it on the light side. I was a mid-level manager, not the Queen of Sheba, so cannons and an honour guard would seem excessive.

By engaging in this, I am assuming that there might be people interested in attending—a giant leap for me. Would 10 chairs be realistic, or would five suffice? Could my mom just bring her teapot from home? And what about the inevitable slide show—should the perm years be included, or should I just forewarn everyone now that many of those photos were inexplicably destroyed in my zealous drive to rid myself of earthly goods in advance of our move?

Of course, booking a venue is problematic as the precise timing is undetermined. It's probably not fiscally prudent to hold a venue for the next six months, so someone else may have to sort out that tiny detail. In any event, this gives me something to think about in between packing for our move and wondering where the dog's water dishes should go. Shame I won't be around to evaluate its success and pick up some tips for next time—but maybe someone can try to let me know how it turned out!

The Keys to the Castle

My sister confessed to me recently that there was a particular date—November 29th, to be exact—when she came to the same sad conclusion that I have mused about in these pages. Namely, that there was a strong possibility that I simply wouldn't make it to this day: the day Kirk and I are to receive the keys to our new wee home.

At that time, the symptoms of my kidney disease had become so debilitating that there wasn't a moment of the day when I didn't feel sick and in pain. Fast-forward to now, a month into receiving more aggressive support for those symptoms and weekly visits from my lovely home care nurses, and I feel transformed. Having moved on from run-of-the-mill pain relief to the stronger palliative drugs, I can now devote at least the morning hours to functioning as a normal human being. I can get things done and see people in small windows; things that once seemed beyond me. My family calls to ask how I am hanging in, and I will say in a clear, strong voice, "I am excellent," and mean it. Because all of these hours in which I have been able to look past my own decline, I treasure in a way that is hard for me to articulate. It is not denial about where I am or what I know is to come, but just a deep appreciation for any time I can spend right now really being present with the people I love.

This is not to say that there haven't been bad days in which the sadness of it all can't help but leak out. Those are as necessary as breathing. They need to happen. They are part of this story. But through it all, I can feel all of my relationships deepening, becoming richer, the connections so much stronger than I had once dreamed possible.

As weird as it may sound, I wouldn't have missed one minute of it. It was meant to be this way. It is what I deserved. And I say that not in a voice of judgment, but a voice of appreciation for what I might have missed had these things not come to pass in quite the manner that they have.

So this afternoon, with the power of my will and my own two feet, I will receive those keys and step through the doors of what will be in a few short weeks our new home and sanctuary. I will walk through the empty spaces and imagine what it will feel like when it is holding all of the remaining possessions that I truly treasure.

Everything I have worked toward will come to pass. It is meant to be. It is a gift; one of so many that have come to me in these past months. As Maya Angelou has said: "The ache for home lives in all of us. The safe place where we can go as we are and not be questioned." It is not the structure itself, or its amenities, but the people and pets who surround me that will make it so.

January
2014

Achieving Perfection and the Art of Futile Pursuits

Part of the challenge, for me, in life as a palliative patient is facing the fact that there are many things about the physical process that I am going through that are beyond my control.

Identifying symptoms and making efforts to treat those symptoms is hard enough, but when it all gets mixed in with a major life event like moving, the lines get blurry. My efforts to plan each element down to the hour sometimes get jumbled with other decisions I make in an attempt to make things "perfect"—and to do it all in a time frame that from the outside may seem unrealistic.

All of the extra energy required to get things done—which I can only assume I will have at any given moment—is taking a toll. There are moments when my body says, "Enough—you have gone too far, and it is time to stop."

I have realized that the longer I live with the uncontrollable nature of this disease, the more rigid I am when any wrinkles appear in my best-laid plans. As a result, those moments when I feel overwhelmed by it all take an equal toll on the people I love, who are valiantly trying to help me through it.

I need to remind myself it is time to let it go, trusting that everything will work out as it should, that none of these trivial issues is insurmountable in the grand scheme of things.

I have always been a person who takes the time to sort out how I am really feeling at any given moment. I ask myself why it is so important that everything must be perfect. Why do I feel the need to try to spare everyone any effort, to try to do it all myself?

In some ways I suppose it comes down to the fact that if I stop for even one minute, I fear that I won't be able to start again. I have no time for a do-over, and making the new space perfect is my flawed way of trying to make sure that everything will be OK when I am gone. That it won't matter if I am missing from the picture if the scenery is in good shape.

. . . .

FRIDAY, JANUARY 3

A Funny Thing Happened on the Way to the Crematorium

Planning one's own funeral is not unlike planning a wedding. This is something I personally have never done, but I am given to understand there are many lists involved. People get rather maniacal trying to decide where to seat the relatives they don't care for, and with whom.

My lovely binder of information that now resides on my dining room table from the palliative care at home program contains all sorts of checklists and helpful resources, including a list of local funeral homes. Somehow during the visit from my home care nurse yesterday the question came up of whether or not I had picked one.

As I have never found the prospect of being six feet under particularly appealing, I prefer the thought of cremation—less baggage to manage for all concerned. One name struck me in an odd way. "Simply Cremations" offers a lower-cost version of what I would have assumed to be a rather straightforward process, eschewing the bells and whistles that I would have thought would seem inappropriate for such an event in any case.

Though it certainly is descriptive, the name struck me as a bit utilitarian, bringing to mind other products that might be more aptly named this way: "Simply Tires," "Simply Ratchets," "Simply Buttons." Perhaps other names were considered and then tossed out: "No Frills Cremations," "Cremations for Less" or "Cremation Liquidation Warehouse."

Having said all that, I am always one for a bargain—and in the scheme of things am not likely to complain about lack of customer service after the fact. I suppose I could let someone else troll through the list, but one likes to be prepared—and pick the dignified choice.

....

SUNDAY, JANUARY 5
Silver Linings

I was never a particularly joyous person. Over the years, my "glass-half-empty" world-view only became more entrenched, first in journalism, where sad or infuriating stories dominated the landscape (with the occasional good-news story thrown in as a filler), and then in the world of health communications, where the myriad "issues" plaguing that sector often trump its breakthroughs, heroines and triumphant success stories.

I have always been a worrier, armed with a powerful imagination that would contort the simplest endeavours into some sort of ordeal as a matter of course.

While that style of thinking still lives in me, I find myself in these past months opening myself up further and further to the wonder of life. Even at this late stage, I marvel at what it feels like to have love in your heart, simply experiencing connection with other people without mentally leaping to what they "really think about me" or poisoning it with assumed ulterior motives.

The small exchanges and events of the day fill me with a happiness that is almost alien in its intensity. Something inside me radiates appreciation for every gift big and small: a kind word, an unexpected note, a reminder of the past that isn't clouded by the sadness of other parts of the story.

I have had months to absorb this process and move into this place; to limit the fear that still lives in the bad days, and to understand that those thoughts are fleeting and not by any measure the bulk of this story.

I think about what it must be like for people who don't have the time to make this kind of shift in perspective. Despite all the physical symptoms and indignities of my failing kidneys, I am grateful to have to come to this place. Since my diagnosis, I have regained some of the wonder and joy that I never really stopped long enough to experience, or allowed myself to feel. I am ripping off, inch by inch, the badge of fatalism that once clouded all that is good.

While my physical self is not healing, my heart is in a state of long-overdue repair. I am clearing out the cobwebs of what has been, and opening up to the wonder of being loved now. The joy of small moments, the growing acceptance of the opportunities this experience has brought; and the people it has brought me back to . . . I simply could not imagine ending my days without reverently holding these gifts in my hands and being thankful.

A Drain on the System

I can't help but reflect, sometimes, on what it costs to care for someone like me, and how fortunate I am that because of where I live, the direct costs I have faced through this journey so far are limited. After spending much of my working life in and around the health-care system, I don't need to be reminded about the cost of care, nor do I take for granted the resources I am using when I run into trouble.

On the balance sheet so far, I know I have not been a significant drain, partly because I'm able to manage reasonably self-sufficiently, and partly because I have chosen "comfort measures" over the more aggressive options available.

I try very hard not to feel guilty about expressing that I need help sometimes. Since receiving regular check-ins and medication support from a nurse through Island Health's palliative care at home program, I have been spared costly hours in the ER (where I landed several times in the past months when my symptoms overcame me). But I worry that as budgets tighten in the ever-pressing and demanding world of acute care, programs like this might be at risk.

The irony, of course, is that programs like this one reduce the burden on hospitals by keeping people like me functioning and supported at home. But social programs simply don't seem high on the priority list these days, even though as citizens of Canada, we blithely expect to have access to more and more resources as we age. These values we hold dear in our personal lives—to care for and support each other and the ones we love—often seem to have dropped off the public radar.

Maybe it is true that we only really begin to care about such things when we, or someone we know or love, find ourselves dangling, waiting for a solution that may not exist. Maybe I am just really grateful that right now I have this incredible gift; caring professionals who treat me gently, with empathy, and who offer such life-altering support. Maybe I am just afraid that at some point in the future, someone like me may not have the same option available to them; that they may be forced to face this journey from the discomfort of a hospital bed, not surrounded by the things and people they love.

. . . .

From the earliest moments of childhood
I have lived in the shadow of death
It has hung over my life
Till it seems like all I do is wait
For those dark moments to come

. . . .

THURSDAY, JANUARY 9
The Seed

During the summer after my final year in elementary school, I developed a passion for tennis. I loved the power, the feel of the racket in my hand and the "thwack" of the ball against it, even when I was just practising, hitting the ball over and over again against a cement wall on the left side of the school I had just escaped.

The previous four school years had been particularly miserable ones. I had changed schools and neighbourhoods at the end of Grade 3, leaving behind a core group of friends. In my new school I found myself injected into an already cliquey collection of girls in what are arguably some of the more awkward years of the transition out of childhood.

The fact I was as round as I was tall was not a huge plus in my favour—and I spent an inordinate amount of time trying and failing to gain hold in the closed social circles that existed. At that age, there is a significant amount of what parents would refer to as teasing, which now would fall under the category of bullying. On many days, the prospect of setting foot in the school door would fill me with anxiety to the point of making myself sick and begging to stay home when morning came.

The other day, while thumbing through the pages of a diary I kept at the time, I discovered a little note on orange paper stuffed in a corner. When I unfolded it, I saw, in small letters, the words "some days I really hate myself." That feeling, and the fact that I wanted to hide that thought in a little folded note, made me cry.

So when Grade 7 was over and the prospect of junior high school was not yet fully dominating my thoughts, tennis became the perfect outlet to exorcise some of my pent-up anger and frustration. By the end of the summer I could hold my own with some of my sister's older friends who as a courtesy offered to take me out on the court.

It altered me in some big and small ways. And then came the moment toward the end of the summer when my mom took me shopping for back-to-school clothes, and we ran into an acquaintance of hers in the now-defunct Woodward's department store. This woman was someone we both found rather intimidating; an effect that very stylish aggressive women seemed to hold over both of us. After looking at me up and down, she remarked to my mom how much weight I had lost and how much better I looked.

It was innocuous enough as remarks go—and probably true, given my increased exercise. Getting a little bit taller that summer probably further enhanced the effect. But that remark stuck with me for years. While I stuffed academic awards earned in school under my bed as if they were dust mites meant to annoy me, that carrot—that potential to be recognized in that way that all the teen magazines and TV shows held up as crucially important—held me captive. Thin was beautiful and anything else was unacceptable.

It seems so wrong that one stupid remark from someone who didn't particularly care for me should have that kind of power—power that I willingly gave away along with what was left of my self-worth.

. . . .

THURSDAY, JANUARY 9
The Trouble With Pronouncements

Just when I stop droning on about my self-sufficiency, my body decides it is going to stop co-operating. Being abundantly honest, I am in tremendous pain today. Several of the signs that my kidney failure is getting worse are flaring up, the day before we are due to move into our new home.

Some of the medications that helped me get through that burst of activity prior to the holidays are starting to lose steam, meaning I must take bigger doses over shorter periods. And now, to add to the indignity, there are signs that the toxins that are no longer being filtered out are painfully depositing in my joints, meaning I am barely able to walk.

Of course I managed to pack two boxes before 7 a.m., before I came to my senses and retired to the couch. I also spoke to my lovely family doctor who will check in with the specialist to determine what, if anything, can be done.

It is discouraging as there is so much I wanted to accomplish today and I want to rail at my body for the bad timing. Fortunately, I have plenty of helping hands and have to try very hard to allow them to do what needs to be done without jumping up to intervene. Not one of my stronger suits! So today, while again counting my blessings, I will let my body be what it is and hope this pain is short-lived.

. . . .

It's Not All About Me

One thought that is very present for me right now is the way in which my rough days affect the people who are closest to me, particularly my immediate family. So desperate are they to take away the pain, ease the road and spare me from upset, that sometimes it becomes a weight in its own right to reassure them that they've done enough.

They express their love and concern in very different ways—as different as their own natures and experiences. It is hard not to sense some anguish on their part when they confront the fact that nothing they have done or said can erase this problem; when the "I love you" at the end of the conversation seems harder to declare.

I am also learning painful lessons about the delicate nature of changes in medication. One such change resulted in the return—with a vengeance—of symptoms that that particular drug was supposed to be combating. This meant more time with a home care nurse—a huge drain on my family doctor's precious time—all while movers were hauling our belongings from our old home to the new one.

I was fortunate that my sister took me in, wrapped me in blankets with a bucket nearby, rubbed my back and held my head in her hands when things got out of control. These most intimate gestures are ones that as adults and sisters we would normally never share. She had to spend yet more time away from her job—to leap up and get me water, field calls from the doctor's office, rush to the drugstore for yet more new prescriptions and hold my hand.

Meanwhile, my mom, dad, Kirk and Miranda did a tremendous amount of work—so much so that when I finally made it to the new house last night, everything appeared as if we had lived here for years. It is so very beautiful, I pinch myself as I walk through the rooms—everything I imagined has come true.

And none of it would have happened without the arms, the strength, the incredible hard work of my family. It really doesn't mean anything that they show it in different ways because our love is so much stronger than that.

. . . .

SATURDAY, JANUARY 11
What a Difference a Day Makes

One affirming visit from my home nurse Joan, a check-in from my amazing family doctor (note it was a Saturday!) and I'm back on track with my medication and feeling so much better than I have in days. After a catch-up nap came a homemade dinner that I actually had the energy to make myself in our lovely new kitchen.

Over the past few days the story had taken such a violent turn for the worse that I truly wondered if I would make it to this new home, or whether the time had come for me to go to hospice.

I held my sister's hand at the worst moments and said that maybe my body was trying to tell me that this is the end, while tears dripped from our eyes.

But as the ever-wise nurse Joan reminded me today, for patients like me, the roller-coaster may go up and down, and a couple of days on the down slope is not necessarily an affirmation that ascension is not also possible—words that I truly needed to hear this morning.

So I could stop exclaiming how happy I am at this moment, but I can't help myself. These days are a treasure, a precious gift. I savour these moments with every fibre of my being. Knowing how the alternative feels only makes this day sweeter.

What constitutes a great day is shifting as this journey rolls along. Right now, two wee dogs recline on either side of me, counting rabbits in their dreams. We are in a space we all adore. We are comfortable and feel not a single pang of sorrow for what we have left behind. Ready to build whatever memories time allows us, in a space that feels exactly like home, our sweet wee oasis that on so many levels was meant to be. So carry me up, Mr. Roller-Coaster. Strap me in and let's go.

. . . .

MONDAY, JANUARY 13
Let's Make Believe

Some days, in between injections and pills and symptom searching, one must just turn one's back on all things connected to the world of palliative care, throw your hands in the air, suspend reality and just shop with your sister. It is good simply to wander around stores as if you haven't just turned your back on all things material, and pretend for a moment that you are back where you were before, with nothing but time stretching before you.

Ignore any clues that things might be less than sunny. Force yourself out of your pyjamas and re-enter society as if nothing has changed—as if a tornado hasn't whipped through your mind, body and soul. Find genuine interest in the cute shoes displayed in a store window. Hug your sister as if you have endless days to repeat this pattern—a year from now, 10 years from now, infinite togetherness (where schedules permit).

It is a pretence we can both happily indulge in—though careful that we don't "overdo it," drinking in the moment as greedily as a glass of wine after a miserable day in the "before" time.

Who knew how much we really love one another? I suppose I thought I did—but now I have irrefutable evidence that there is nothing she would not do for me, give to me, or sacrifice for me. What one might assume to be true is as real as her hand reaching out to hold mine, catching me when I was too weak to stand, and saying with her beautiful blue eyes everything I ever wanted to hear her say. My "K," my love.

· · · · · · · · · ·

THURSDAY, JANUARY 16
When the Whirlwind Ends

In less than three and a half months I have sold a house and found a new place, eliminated more than half of my possessions in a de-cluttering frenzy, lived through showings and cleaning and staging, celebrated Christmas, endured endless appointments, met with lawyers and bankers, arranged all of the details around our move from utilities to the moving company, helped set up the new house, made all of the necessary changes to ensure when we downsized Kirk could carry on mortgage-free, paid off my Smart car, lived through medication changes and adjustments, had good days and scary days, wrote an advance care plan and completed my will, and planned an entire service for after I pass, including writing the program and lining up who will speak. I had a magical last fling in Toronto, where I spent time with Kirk's amazing kids, their partners, little ones, and my dear friend Shae and his lovely bride-to-be Sara. I learned Kirk's daughter was expecting her first child. I connected with dozens of people from my past and present through the magic of this medium. And I have written my final blog post, to be shared by my sister at some point in the future.

Some days, I honestly didn't think I would get through it all. The prospect that I might leave unfinished business behind terrified me, leaving me shaking and sobbing at the thought of it—a terror that, try as they might, my loved ones could not lift from me.

But now I can only marvel at how it somehow all came together. It is time to let these things go and find a different sense of purpose for the days that remain.

As I reflect on everything that has happened and all the items checked off on my lists, I feel my heart bursting with a sense of overwhelming gratitude and love. While I did do some of it alone, I owe bigger debts to the people who have been there for me than I could ever adequately repay. Had I not had the benefit of Kirk and my family holding my hand, I know I would not be where I am in this moment—reflecting with awe on how healing this journey has been, discovering parts of myself and the ones I love that I might have missed entirely had things not unfolded as they ultimately did.

It has taken facing the prospect of death to find my light and my life. I have felt the healing of so many parts of myself that I once believed to be incurable.

Had someone written this script for me I would have mocked it completely—yet here I sit, arms open wide to the world, saying simply, if this is life, bring it on.

. . . .

FRIDAY, JANUARY 17
Rolling in the Deep

Every part of this journey has a flavour; a tone. There are times when reaching out is desirable and achievable, and times when it is necessary to retreat. Times when the body shouts and others when it merely murmurs. Times when the mind supersedes the body, and times when it is undone by it all. Times when the gravity of this comes back to me in the form of my monthly blood-work reports; the follow-up calls; the underlying knowledge that this roller-coaster ride continues on with its dips and turns. I ride it blind, with only the wrenching of this piece or that to tell me where I am.

As the weight of all of the self-imposed activity of recent months lifts from my shoulders—and Kirk generously picks up an ever-heavier load—we are finding our way to a new equilibrium, more aligned than we have been on this path before. This renewed connection was necessary for both of us. It allows me, little by little, to do what I need to do to let go. I am depleted, it is true, but more at peace now. My mind is not racing, just soaking in the moments of the day deliberately wherever possible. I am feeling calm, feeling the connection of my family ever closer, more in tune with where I am, feeling deeply loved. I am rolling in it now, quite gently, but with purpose and intention. Closing out the other noise, my hands looser now on the bars of this ride . . . just rolling.

. . . .

SATURDAY, JANUARY 18
Attention-Seeking?

There is a phrase I have referenced before in these pages—"attention-seeking behaviour"—that is frequently ascribed to people living with eating disorders or any other manner of addiction or mental illness. Deeply dismissive and paternalistic, it is a phrase I heard frequently from health professionals in the context of both my working life and my own personal journey.

Clearly this phrase has gnawed at me, frequently making me question my own motivation for sharing these stories in such a public way. When I worked in the Ministry of Health, it was often thrown out when eating disorder patients, in desperation, would take their stories to the media, desperate for access to the treatment they believed would help them regain their health.

Having had much time for reflection, I have come to the conclusion that it exemplifies how the clinical approach to mental illness remains mired in the Dark Ages in so many ways. While technology, new interventions and ever-growing investments in acute care have all but drowned out more community-based supports and prevention efforts, our overwhelming discomfort with diseases of the mind as opposed to the body ensures that this obscene imbalance is one that will take decades to overcome—if it is overcome at all. Research, support for new medication alternatives, and treatment approaches for eating disorders remain limited and depressingly low on our priority list, despite the billions invested in our healthcare system each year.

Which brings me back to the foul notion that any health professional would continue to dismiss the more blatant cries for help by using language like "attention-seeking" that so summarily dismisses the message being sent. We are here by the legions, and the time for better alternatives is long past. We will not stand for being treated as the lepers of the patient hierarchy. What we need, in a word, is help.

For Rachael

I received a note last night from Rachael, a former colleague generous enough to follow along with these musings and to provide the most wonderful notes of support and love to me privately in recent months.

She wrote to describe a recent trip to her gym, where over time she has noticed a client working out on a particular piece of equipment in a manner that was more manic than normal. Having observed the pronounced diminishing size of the client over a relatively short time, she thought of my story and wondered what, if anything, she should do to express her concern.

Back in the days when support groups were something I attempted to participate in, I heard about situations in which eating-disordered clients had been physically banned from certain gyms by management concerned about their well-being (not to mention the liability the gyms could expose themselves to if in the course of one of these "manic" workouts a clearly vulnerable client was injured in pursuit of their goal). These interventions were deeply felt by the clients in question, and served as important messages in overcoming the denial that surrounds these illnesses.

But two things struck me about this exchange with my former colleague. First, the profound impulse of caring she felt toward a complete stranger who she could see was likely in a danger zone in a scenario in which most people might simply look away. Second, if I had not shared my story in as honest a way as I could, this observation may not have occurred in the first place, nor the question of whether some action on her part might be helpful for a woman wasting away.

While I don't know where any of this will lead, I do know that sometimes a cry for help can only be heard if your ears are open to receive it. As members of this village that is humanity, we all share the responsibility to act in as sensitive a manner as we can when we see someone at risk—a charge that not every mortal soul has the willingness to meet.

So this morning, to Rachael I send my most profound love and gratitude for your bravery, your insight, and the capacity of your huge and open heart. And to the woman you described, I send my sincere hope that she has a hand to reach out to when the running stops.

. . . .

Denial is Not Just a River in Egypt

If it strikes you, reading this, that the manifestations of this palliative experience can turn on a dime—from days of glory to days that seem to take too long to end—then you would be right.

Generally speaking, mornings seem better than afternoons— but that doesn't always hold true. Sometimes I go back to that primordial instinct to shut everything and everyone out, to curl into a ball, lick my wounds. And it is on the very worst days that I seem to find it hardest to pick up the phone and ask what, if anything, can be done to make it better.

My lovely home nurse Joan questioned me about that in the gentlest way yesterday. In those moments, my biggest challenge is knowing what to ask for. With all of the medications I already take, which cocktail or next step will truly bring comfort at any given moment, when the ground shifts so frequently and sometimes so unexpectedly? Which symptom will raise its head and knock me down?

We navigate through little challenges, like a prescription that can't be filled quickly enough because genuine shortages continue to exist in the supply chain. Sometimes this means that a drug ordered by my doctor yesterday—through the pharmacy designated for palliative care drugs delivered in the community—can't be filled until after 1 o'clock this afternoon, and some pharmacies can't even access it at all.

All of this has made one thing perfectly clear: As much as I have tried to put the fact I have a terminal illness on the back burner for months now while all of the various activities in my life unfolded, the pretence must come to an end. I can't leap in and out of normal activities anymore because the reckoning, after the fact, is simply too great. As painful as it is for me to be as selfish as I feel right now, I need to really work on better identifying when to call in the cavalry and when to retreat; when to wave the white flag and when to simply breathe through it. In short, I need to learn to ask for help—without necessarily being equipped with my own solution first.

· · · · · · · · · ·

THURSDAY, JANUARY 23
The Business of Dying

The costs associated with the "death industry" now sit at an estimated $1.3 billion and climbing in this country. In other words, it ain't cheap for people to kick the bucket.

The push for an elaborate and costly event that would rival a modern wedding remains very strong for funeral homes across the country. They make a killing promising the bereaved that their departed loved ones will be swathed in the finest of materials (if you really love someone, you wouldn't want to be thrifty about it) and devising elaborate ceremonies worthy of a minor celebrity.

My amazing family physician, who also happens to devote a significant portion of her time and energy to a hospice program, talked to me yesterday about some of the logistics of my own demise and the foundations of the palliative care movement. It advocates for the normalization of death as part of the natural journey of life, rather than seeing it as a distasteful sales opportunity that preys on people's guilt and discomfort with mortality. For me, it was important to choose options that make sense for my family and, more importantly, won't lead anyone to bankruptcy. There will be no elaborate hand-hewn urn collecting more dust on someone's mantle, no silk-lined coffin wrapped in mahogany, no giant stone that says I graced the planet on certain dates. I will have none of it.

The influence of other cultures where approaches to death and its rituals seem infinitely more civilized can only help to enlighten our view of death as part of the human experience. Why is it necessary, in this country, to incur a cost to have Aunt Mary's body dragged to a crematorium or funeral home, or face the third degree and endless forms for transporting the body yourself, if you are able? It's all part of the politics of keeping death shrouded in some mysterious netherworld that only those in the business of it could possibly navigate.

Making decisions about your wishes (and budgeting accordingly) also saves the ones who love you from facing the pressure of such decisions when they are grieving, which one hopes will be their only job, after the fact.

. . . .

THURSDAY, JANUARY 23
Settling

There has always been a negative tone to the word "settling," implying that one has stopped striving for something better. We thought, when we took the step of selling our house to find something more suitable for our changing circumstances, that this move would represent the ultimate in settling—a sign of some failure. And yet, here we are in our new space, and regardless of the physical challenges I have faced recently, I can say I have never been happier or more at peace since we "settled" for this beautiful haven, this quiet oasis.

From the back deck off the dining room, my view is a beautiful cedar tree alive with a band of squirrels who entertain me with their twitching noses, dive-bombing through the branches. From my living room couch I see only a sea of green. I sleep deeply, breathe deeply, try to take in the peace. This afternoon the dogs and I lay down separately on the living room floor. We basked in the sunlight pouring through the sun-deck door, content to feel the warmth flow over us. I haven't set foot in the old house since moving day, and have no desire to do so. I said goodbye, and that is enough. People who have visited us in both spaces genuinely say that this place is better—something we don't need to be told. So our wee townhouse is in no way what we settled for. It is the space where we are, very happily, settling in.

. . . .

FRIDAY, JANUARY 24
There is No 'I' in Team

For the people who stand in the circle closest to me, the evolution of my illness in recent months has meant navigating uncharted waters. The question of who is doing what and when, regarding my growing dependence, is sometimes confounded by actions that misfire, and misinterpretation. The fact is, while I feel pretty confident in my relationships with each of them as individuals, that familiarity doesn't necessarily translate to the relationships they must now forge with one another in this new context.

While they are obviously not strangers to one another, neither have they ever shared much more than what was communicated through me. So even as they are processing their own experience in witnessing this passing, they have new responsibilities and boundaries to add to their plate.

Watching them flounder through it, from my perch not fully on the sideline, is just one of the new challenges that comes with this territory. To their credit, they have more than risen to the occasion, treating me and one another with incredible generosity and caring. And I have my own culpability in all of this, having not done a better job of fostering that feeling of a family united over the years. The end result is just deeper love—a different kind of tenderness that we feel in recognizing our own unique quirks and sensibilities.

I now truly know what it is to depend on the kindness of people who are not strangers—people who feel an obligation to me that is easy to take for granted. These moments bring new opportunities for learning and growth. I try to quell an ingrained instinct for control, quiet my urge to intervene, and allow "the team" to do their work.

. . . .

SATURDAY, JANUARY 25
Time

I think of each day differently now. Time is compartmentalized into hours and minutes. How many of those will fall into the category of some semblance of normal, and how many will go off the rails? How much activity is too much—and when will sleep come and take it away?

I inhale the "good hours," steep in their intoxicating vapours. I cling to each comfortable moment for as long as it lasts, until some other feeling creeps in; a sickness in the belly, a wave of fatigue rolling in like fog through my body.

My frame of reference is changing. I exhale through those other times, clinging to the memory of ease when the picture shifts, only hanging on to what was solid and good. What represents success is a loosely constructed picture, unrecognizable from a past that is gradually slipping away until there is only this present, this collection of hours and minutes passing.

. . . .

I will tell you why
These painful secrets mean so much
All the intrigue of this hidden life
Which is all I have that's mine
That none of you have touched
And made your impressions
To scare me away
The excuses spill out my mouth
That I prepared far in advance
And the anguish I endure with you
Is forgettable when compared to
The victory of pulling the wool over
My own eyes

. . . .

SUNDAY, JANUARY 26
How Long Has This Been Going On?

It was never entirely a secret; my eating disorder. My family was certainly more than aware of it from an early age. Some people in my life knew it was there, and others merely suspected. Later in my career I would sometimes make reference to a "past issue" with journalists I worked with, but never without also suggesting that it was all over now. An outright lie.

The issue truly came to a head when a small group of adult, long-time sufferers got together to formally approach the media and the minister to beg for help with the fact that they were still struggling, decades into their battle. As I worked in the communications world in the Health Ministry at that time, this issue struck many uncomfortable chords. The part of me that was in denial bought into the patient-blaming kind of language and behaviour that often represented step one of "managing" such an issue.

Of course, privately, I identified to the core with the depth of their pain; their longing to be well, their debilitating shame, the cycle of failed promises to loved ones to "fix" it. Most of all, I identified with their deeply ingrained resistance to experiencing any consequences of what that fix might entail—the rising of those numbers on the scale that would represent a failure of control. We might be prepared to confront it, but not prepared to give up the fear that ending the disorder might uncage some monstrous hunger.

I was always seeking some magical approach that would—without any serious work on my part—slay the beast but allow me to maintain the compliment-inspiring state of thinness that our society remains obsessed with. Others slaved at the gym, ate and then bemoaned whatever calorie-rich snack they had just consumed, and made resentful remarks about how I stayed less than obese. Meanwhile, I was scouting for bathrooms that would grant me enough privacy to rid myself of everything I consumed when I could hold out no longer, when the deprivation had run its course. I was literally, as the saying goes, having my cake and eating it too—and promptly getting rid of it.

The longer the abnormal becomes normal, the tougher it is to beat—not impossible, but certainly the odds are not good. So it is no real surprise that I should find myself where I am today, trying to make peace with this monster, letting it know "you may have won but you didn't take my soul." The part of me you couldn't beat is still breathing—faintly, slowly, but still here.

· · · · · · · · · ·

MONDAY, JANUARY 27

We Are Not Hangers

I have a small, framed picture on my dresser entitled "We Are Not Hangers."

Its message is that we are so much more than a mortal frame on which to hang clothing. Nothing exemplifies the reason for this message more than the arrival of jeans as a fashion trend when I was coming of age.

When I was 10 or 11 years old, my mom bought me my first pair of Wrangler jeans. I couldn't tell you the size. I only know that with that one purchase, I suddenly felt that I would belong, would be like all of the other girls, abandoning the polyester blends for good and never looking back.

There was only one "good" jeans store at the mall in Prince George. Pine Centre Mall was the centre of the universe as far as my compatriots and I were concerned. The denim store inside had been designed like some kind of western town, with wooden floors and stacks and racks of jeans as far as the eye could see.

By the time I started shopping there, size mattered—big time. We always knew what size the popular girls wore because it was frequently discussed. In fact, the number was often visible on the exterior label. So while jeans were considered an essential item, the exercise of purchasing them was always an excruciating one because I knew, in my pre-eating-disorder days, that I was a good four or five inches broader around the waist than the waifs I admired most. To add insult to injury, the store did not have any mirrors in the changing rooms—nor was the change-room area separated from main store, where other teenagers would gather, some on a similar mission, some simply there to pass the time, gawking and whispering.

I would sheepishly and angrily pile up pairs of jeans on the little stool inside the changing room. With each pair I tried on I would emerge, humiliated, zipper scraped up over belly, tummy bound like an old Chinese woman's foot, standing awkwardly in front of the nearest mirrored surface I could find, trying not to burst into tears when I would see how awful they looked. I wasn't at all like the models sporting Calvin Klein in the ads that were all over teen magazines and television at the time. Nervously I would glance around to see if someone who knew me from school might be watching, ready to report back through the gossip wires about seeing the ugly girl at the mall with her hideous body.

I didn't know at the time that there would never be a number small enough. That goal after goal would be exceeded with no sense of victory, no feeling of accomplishment—just a yearning for it to go a little bit lower.

I ask myself now why size trumped soul, trumped heart, trumped love. These are numbers that just don't ever add up.

....

TUESDAY, JANUARY 28
When

I think you would forgive me for confessing that, as much as I try every minute of every hour not to "go there," the urge to ruminate on when my end will come is so very powerful.

I have read up on what to expect when you are dying of kidney failure and some of it definitely feels applicable, while other markers are not part of the picture yet.

Nothing about this has been entirely predictable as time frames and deadlines once held out as "likely" have since shifted and passed. I want to be above it all—just let it flow and all that—but that is easier said than done when you have endless hours with nothing to occupy you but your own thoughts, circling.

My own doctor, with her expertise in palliative medicine, reminds me that even she has no answer. Ultimately, the body answers the question for us, though admittedly certain things you do or don't do can speed things along.

For awhile now I have been stubbornly carrying on through dates and events I wanted to experience, to achieve some of my final goals before I pass. Yesterday was one of those milestones: We signed the final transaction papers on the sale of our former home. As of this Friday, the proceeds will be deposited to our account and I will be able to say that we own our new place free and clear of a mortgage—a goal I frankly never believed could be realized in my lifetime.

As each day passes I become more aware of what comes next, wondering where my body will take me from here. There is nothing seemingly essential ahead—a few "to-do's" with respect to finishing touches on our new place, but no big goals to define the coming weeks for me. Except, of course, for the sharing of time and love with people I treasure, as my energy will allow—generally not in person, but in many other ways that still matter to me and are not insignificant.

I want to derive whatever I can from this; take away memories not too clouded by the prospect of what awaits me physically.

There's still time to keep writing my way through it, step by step, word placed next to word. Pandora's box open and gaping, flying sentences that weave around me, waiting for the story to continue, and careful not to ask (please don't ask) "for how long?"

Hunger

When you live for decades with an eating disorder you have a lot of time to think about the topic of hunger. There is the physical sensation, of course, which can feel like a constant presence in your head and in your body. But then there is the question: hungry for what?

Now, I can say I was hungry for experience, for love, for connection; to scream and cry and run without self-consciousness, to walk down the street without feeling one thousand eyes sizing me up and finding me lacking. Hungry to tear out of, in the words sung by the now late, great Pete Seeger, "little boxes made out of ticky-tacky and they all look just the same..." To forge some alternative life without conforming—shutting up—being a girl.

I hungered to be different, to stand out, to be heard—oh Lord, to be heard. I felt like there was so much I wanted to say, needed to say, and no way to express it—that I would never be able to get it all out. I hungered to be honest and say, "no, no, no" and, "yes, yes, yes." I hungered to be challenged, to be bowed down by those tasks, to have adventures and to be a risk-taker. To go places. To get out.

At the same I hungered to just stay home, keep my thoughts to myself, be like everyone else, have the life I was supposed to want. To strive for marriage, leading to children, leading to... where would it lead? I hungered to be faithful and devout and to believe what I was taught and not question everything and everyone, and wonder what they were thinking all the time, to a point of madness or obsession.

I hungered to be healthy, to slay the beast that was slowly replacing my life, not face a constant dilemma of how I could do anything—go to school, go to work, go on a trip—without taking it with me every single day. To spend just one hour of my life not thinking about it, or perhaps two days free of the numbers and the magnetic pull of the scale, with its power to dictate what I thought about myself in any given moment.

I was hungry to be thin, rail-thin, skeletal. Bones clicking on bones, sinew on sinew. To be beautiful—devastatingly and heart-stoppingly so. Hungry for power. Talent. To be clever. For submission. Hungry for meaning, a reason to be here, to know why it was this way—and why it couldn't be different. Why I couldn't have just been born somebody else.

Hungry to be myself, to be satisfied, to feel sated and content and not full of the bad. Radiating peace, radiating light. Hungry for all those impossible, contradictory things, all at once, all at the same time, all day, every day, every hour. That is my hunger.

. . . .

The very walls that surround me are not safe
From my open mouth
The boards nailed down on the floor can
Not escape
This gaping hole
This ravenous heart
This searing hunger.
It gnaws at my television
Cramping for the things it cannot have.
It drowns the couch
In salivatory juices.
It will not be quenched
By my disgust
Your feeble protest
Your open eyes
Watching this progression
Steeped in your shame

Your impotent rage
It only serves to
Spur me on
Cheerleader to my madness

. . . .

Drugs At What Cost?

When I was going through one of my rougher patches around the time of our move and there was difficulty controlling the constant pain, I was prescribed a steroid—a "super-drug"—for three days. By day three, I felt the surge of my energy return. I could function, leave the house, hold a conversation, spend at least part of the day almost escaping from this reality; the debilitating nausea, the throbbing in my joints. Then it stopped and a version of my previous state began to settle in, my body resisting movement, food, conversation.

This temporary conversion was like stopping the path of my illness—dare I say some version of normal. But every silver lining has its cloud. I discussed this drug with my home care nurse and my doctor last week. The question being, should I try it one more time?

My doctor was quick to advise that while there is no doubt that this drug has its benefits, powerfully felt in some patients, the longer you are on it, the greater the impact of long-term steroid use is felt. There would be changes in my body and face, bloating, difficulty settling down, and many other side-effects that I won't go into. But the power of those three days was so intoxicating, so altering, that it was impossible for me to say anything else but "give me more."

Now I am another four or five days into it and yes, many of those benefits are being felt, I will not lie. I have more energy—I was able to make dinner yesterday, able to leave the house. But I am also noticing more disturbing effects that I must have missed the first time. I feel a certain restlessness, an inability to be still or to settle down. I am short-tempered, and agitated. It is harder to sleep.

I can't help wondering what I am doing. What am I delaying by staying this course? Has anything about this progression really been altered, or am I simply delaying the moment when the reckoning will be felt? Is this a comfort measure or something entirely different? Is it what I really want in my heart, to falsely drag this out this way?

I honestly don't know the answers to these questions. What do I really want from this, and for how long? That is the question that hangs over all the pills I am taking. At what point do I just say: "enough"? There really is no utility to this anymore. They are not a cure. They will not stop this; won't make a material difference. How much more do I have to do before saying: "enough"?

. . . .

THURSDAY, JANUARY 30
Push, Pull

I have to be honest here. I am in a weird space right now, which is why I find myself writing at 3:30 a.m.

I can't quite put my finger on it, but I feel a bit undone by the upheaval in my life patterns right now, which have largely been tossed out the window.

My best guess is that I must be feeling a bit of a rebellion against the intimacy that seems to accompany my current state. My openness has compelled many people to message me privately and engage with me in ways well outside the comfort zone of someone who lived so many years locked in her own secrets. Privacy was synonymous with shutting away the world.

This even applies to those who might be considered close to me. I am unaccustomed to their desire to check in as frequently as they do now, always with the increasingly dreaded question, "How are you feeling?" Frankly, I am weary of answering it, as it isn't a constant for me—I am OK one minute and doubled over in pain the next. I might say I feel OK—or even "fine"—on a Wednesday at 10 a.m. but by 2 p.m. I could be a mess.

Of course people's interest is coming from their caring hearts, so I feel guilty at the same time for telling them—in the nicest way—to back off.

The simple fact is that every note leaves me feeling compelled to respond, even when that is the last thing I feel like doing. Setting boundaries—which was never within my comfort zone—is becoming necessary. Increasingly, the instances in which I can fake it or respond with some false generosity of affection are waning.

Time keeps passing, as does the sense I have only so much of it, so perhaps some of this is not so unexpected.

I think a lot of it goes back to being thrust into a phase in which everything is so much less clear. The constant activity of recent months, while wearing, was much closer to my "normal pace." Now that so many things have been knocked off the "to-do" list, I am floating directionless. For someone who spent so much of her life operating on overload, finding my purpose right now is not coming to me easily. People have a habit of vowing to "live every moment to the fullest" in times like these, but frankly I don't know what that is supposed to really mean, and wouldn't even know how to begin. So I am just me, trying to get through the days and nights and trying not to beat myself up for it. Trying to find a reason for this interim time.

February
2014

Nobody Knows You When You're Down and Out

If this is like a roller-coaster ride—this evolution of an illness—then Saturday night was the closest I have come to flinging right off of it entirely and into the unknown. It was, in short, the scariest day yet. Worse than what I experienced around our moving day.

It came the day after a visit from my lovely home nurse Joan in which we had jointly declared that things were looking up again, enough to say that this coming week just a phone call would suffice, rather than a home visit.

It started on Saturday morning with flu-like symptoms that escalated throughout the day, and by evening I was incoherent, mumbling, and screaming with frustration. Couldn't find a place to sit, stand or lie down for two minutes that felt comfortable—couldn't settle down, couldn't stop the agitation I felt on an unprecedented level. Crawling out of my skin. Pulling at my hair. Misery piled on misery, piled on frustration and shame.

Getting up and wandering around rooms, up and down stairs, barely able to hang onto the railings, ready to topple at any given moment, shuffling in my weakness and unable to stop. Blankets, fabric...too cold...too hot...everything an irritant.

It took a visit from another home nurse and, near midnight, a member of the palliative care response team with a new drug before I could settle for the night. My sister, not sleeping...Not knowing if I would awaken and the cycle would return.

So yesterday we had another, lengthier visit with two amazing members of the team to sort out how we might stop this from happening again—and a new medication regime to add to the ever-growing list.

Now, a more humbling day of trying to recover. Waking up to a feeling not unlike a bad hangover.

I had considered not sharing this, but again, this is what this journey is about. Heaving into the unexpected and hanging on as best we can.

· · · · · · · · · ·

TUESDAY, FEBRUARY 4
Proximity of Spirit

Physical closeness has never been my thing. I am not and have never been a "huggy" person, and unless I know you very well I would likely recoil at the thought of an embrace.

But these things evolve too. My ideas about what I am and am not inclined to do or be are slowly being rewritten in this uncertain period—this interim time. Perhaps it is part of letting so many secrets go. There is a proximity of spirit that comes with freeing oneself from what was once kept bundled in dark corners inside.

Sometimes a hug involves no hesitation. Freely, willingly and openly given, with no holding in or holding back. An embrace that you feel to the core of your being; heart connected to heart, connected to spirit, connected to soul. Its impression lingers on, like a warm blanket that you can wrap around yourself at any moment merely by thinking of it, remembering.

Nothing anyone could possibly give me would mean as much as those hugs, and the people with whom I have shared them.

. . . .

TUESDAY, FEBRUARY 4
I Want to Be Sedated

Over the river and through the woods to get to the other side . . .

Well, I guess I am on the other side of whatever Saturday night was. In a nutshell, I got some kind of bug and was sick all day, which was exacerbated by a drug I shouldn't have been given. Agitation escalated to some kind of batty fit, followed by two visits by palliative care providers, new medication, and now—well, precisely what now?

On Saturday, when asked by the palliative care response team nurse what my goal was, my answer was "sedation." Total knockout; downright oblivion. And I got my wish.

But now how do I let go of it? I mumble. I "sound sleepy," feel unsteady. I am taking less of the new stuff but it still packs a punch.

Yet I don't want to stop it. I can't afford to go back, whatever toll it takes . . . and the toll is losing something that feels like real life.

Not knowing what this time is supposed to accomplish, I am learning that planning anything big in advance is a fool's errand. There is too much uncertainty attached to the everyday . . . not knowing where I go from here, and too groggy to see the road.

Relax. Nothing is Under Control

I don't know why I picked that title. I guess it has everything to do with where I am right now. Someone I love put it on Facebook: a picture with a caption that read, "Relax. Nothing is under control." I found it oddly comforting because it sort of sums up life for me. I am very slowly absorbing the message.

Now that the latest crisis has passed, having no plans is just about the right tempo for me . . . I'm just rolling along, singing your name, feeling the love, dulling the pain.

Feeling everything is better than nothing. Truly, it is. Better than the knock-out punch, the sweet allure of sedation. Now I want to get up again, move my body. Be more loving. Be awake. Let the tension go . . . I want to feel hands on my back that can take those knots away; knots that represent everything that needs to be released to make room for what has yet to be embraced.

. . . .

WEDNESDAY, FEBRUARY 12
The Prison of Mental Illness

A *New York Times* editorial on the weekend pointed to the devastating lack of community mental health supports in the U.S., and the growing phenomenon of jailing mentally ill men and women in order to get them the treatment they can't access in the outside world.

They cite a Justice Institute report from 2006 that shows the problem is worse for women—approximately three-quarters of female inmates have a diagnosed mental illness.

I suspect if we looked a little closer to home here in Canada, the numbers would be equally depressing. A horrible imbalance continues to grow as the insatiable maw of acute care eats up a growing percentage of our health-care dollars and research funding. Meanwhile, patients facing conditions of the mind largely march along with little support, rejecting outdated treatment options that seem woefully behind compared with the progress we've made in supporting patients in other areas.

I suppose I cling to this soapbox for obvious reasons. But it seems we are more prepared to keep on studying the scope of the problem than we are to actually act on the growing lists of recommendations from special commissions, task forces and community-led inquiries that sit on the shelf.

This point was driven home in a poignant account in the *Victoria Times Colonist* by an officer recounting the story of "Dave"—a man tortured by his addiction and mental health issues. He found himself being shuffled through a system that was not prepared to deal with his behaviour or his resistance to abandoning his crutches and accepting the prospect of rehab.

I know all too well that one cannot be forced to accept help when one is fundamentally not ready. But it leaves me wondering what the answer is. How do we encourage someone without hope to find the will to change? And how long will it take to find it?

· · · · · · · · · ·

FRIDAY, FEBRUARY 14
My Funny Valentine

Sometimes, there are moments when I am so overwhelmed that I literally feel I am falling off the end of the earth and there is nothing, no pill, no antidote, that can calm me. It comes on when I least expect it and is accompanied by significant fear that I won't be able to hold it together—that someone from the outside will have to be called in to rescue me from myself.

Such was my feeling last night. I recognized it early enough that I was able to enlist Kirk to help me through it, breathing with me, rubbing the knots out of my back and my arms, not stopping until I fell into a fitful but welcome sleep. There are so many moments when he has no idea how or if he can make anything "better"—moments when his own fatigue and powerlessness in the face of all of this is palpable.

I suppose we envisioned this scenario would come to us some-day, but in reverse order—that it would be me, not Kirk, playing the role of caregiver.

I wonder how long we can keep this up. How long before I hand over this responsibility to somebody else? Is it time to give serious consideration to whether hospice would be a more appropriate option?

But for today, Valentine's Day, as we both battle an unrelentingly stubborn flu, there will be no such decisions made. There is just a deep appreciation for Kirk, and a thank you for the most meaningful gift he could possibly give me—the gift of his caring, the gift of himself.

· · · · · · · · · ·

TUESDAY, FEBRUARY 18

Questions in the Interim Time

They said it would be weeks.

Now, weeks have passed and, tacking on a week of the flu, there is no sign that it—or I—are prepared to relent quite yet. This "interim time"—this time of not having a clear view of how long this will go on—some days, it weighs on me, taunts me, fills my head and won't let me be.

I know that my view is clouded by this flu, on top of the symptoms I already feel on a daily basis. My resources to overcome it are depleted. I also know that you might wonder how I can wish this time away. But, you see, when you hear "weeks," that is what you mentally prepare for. You look at calendars and wonder at some of the choices you made. If this is what you are to expect, you tend to act accordingly.

But of course, no one has ever really known how long I have. It has been pure speculation, the dates and time frames shifting around me. People say it will be obvious. There will be some sure signs of deterioration. My lovely home care nurse Joan says it is not time—not yet. There have been some declines, but not enough to make me totally dependent.

This news, I should greet with a more generous enthusiasm than I do. Frankly, if someone gave me the option, it would be time to go. If I feel like this now, I don't want to hang on for what is worse. I don't want any more lessons in humility at the moment. I want to scream to the universe, "I get it!"

But I can't distinguish between my flu-induced malaise and all the other feelings and symptoms I experience every day. I can't say that "marginally better" is anything worth shooting for. Of course, that in itself seems like sacrilege—something one shouldn't say out loud.

But feelings come and go. They rarely stay stuck in one place unless you are very obstinate about it. New waves come. The sun will shine. I will try not to think about deadlines that come and go—just manage as best I can with what is left. Try to appreciate where I am and believe, to the extent I can, that it is better than the alternative.

Milestones

We're only human—skin and bones, tissues and organs; all of the inner workings that, like a clock, we don't question. There's an inherent faith that everything inside is doing the job it was meant to do in this complex, amazing system. When parts fail, it always comes as a shock, no matter what has led up to it.

I think of this as I face two major milestones in the coming month: a birthday I still am not entirely confident I will see, and the anniversary of the day I got the fateful phone call telling me that my kidneys were failing and I had to head to the hospital without passing "Go."

It is hard to sum up what this year has been for me. My birthday last year was spent in sheer oblivion, then a few weeks later, a single phone call changed everything. I can only believe that life was meant to unfold this way, with all of the love and lessons that have come from this experience.

And now here we are, unclear about what to expect, needing nothing that money can buy, wanting everything and nothing. Just wanting to be held, babied. . . .

I am not looking back and wishing for what I had, just appreciating that there was a past that held something so much more than pain. A past filled with the faces of people who enriched me, challenged me, tolerated me, and loved me. The soft whisper of voices encouraging me to go forward, stick to my guns, to do the right thing when I could.

Through it all, there is the ever-present hum of the rollercoaster . . . by now, so familiar. My arms in the air, less tentatively than before, still riding.

Time to Step Away

"If you can't say anything nice, don't say anything at all." It's an adage passed on by my mom that I wished I had adhered to more closely throughout the course of my life.

I think of this after another day in which agitation got the best of me. The afternoon was spent pacing aimlessly, unable to find comfort anywhere. After desperately consulting the home care nurse and calling up my family doctor and ingesting anything I could to make it stop, I finally gave myself a shot before passing out around 4 p.m., then woke up in a daze at 6:30 this morning.

There are more of these bad days now. Yet another new plan with new medication is on its way. And I, as always, am searching for the meaning behind this, looking for some kind of sign that I just can't make out from my current vantage point.

It all seems too repetitive now, like a story that should have come to an end with the work of a strong editor. It is time for a break—for some time to absorb this change and to do what is necessary now to prepare for what is to come.

March
2014

SATURDAY, MARCH 1

Mrs. In-Between

It is a home day today, the kind of day when leaving the house is unimaginable.

I woke up feeling fragile. Getting coffee had to involve sitting down with my head in my hands several times just to try to propel myself forward, willing myself not to fall down. Some days just go like this. On the whole, they are better than the awful days of anxiety and panic when nothing seems to calm me. But the feeling of being half-present takes some getting used to . . . I am here, but not here—awake, but not entirely present. I struggle to find words to identify what I want.

It feels like I am going through a long tunnel, and the anticipation of breaking free into the light grows stronger the longer the ride goes on. Any kind of stimulation—light, noise, physical touch—feels suffocating and overwhelming.

I'm doing as well as I can, under the circumstances—as well as anyone would, when your days are numbered but no one can reveal what those numbers are. Levels of engagement and activity are narrowing as this goes on, naturally curtailing where my increasingly limited energy is directed.

I wonder, these days, where is the elusive silver lining? Where is the promise that things will shift again, turning today into a memory that I might one day look back on nostalgically as the "good times"?

It is all about perspective—the lens you choose to look through. Photographic filters to soften the lines, changing the current view into something more palatable. Sepia tones to dull things, to better reflect this place I am in.

. . . .

THURSDAY, MARCH 6

To Sleep, Perchance to Dream

There is a time in a journey when relenting is the only logical option.

Yesterday my amazing home nurse Joan, my family doctor Leah, and a member of the palliative care response team worked with me through my latest crisis—a 13-hour anxiety attack that began at 3 in the morning and that no amount of medication would make go away.

It is clear that the sicker I get, the more rapidly each previously workable medication regime begins to fail, leading to more of these scary days. The latest medical decisions are more drastic— aggressive, even—the goal being to prevent those bad physical and emotional symptoms from creeping back in. We have moved into full-on sedation, every four hours, day and night. Two drugs are to be injected in shifts by my family members, who are sacrificing sleep and their own obligations to be there for me.

I have had to accept that the limits of what any drug can do can change on a dime, and that waiting for an alternative to appear can take time. I am groggy, slurring my words, falling from time to time when I get careless with my movements—but adjusting. I still feel grateful that yesterday is but a bad dream and I can face tomorrow without fear, cocooned in the knowledge that I have a dream team around me to make the way forward easier.

. . . .

So much for spontaneity
My mind is so full of rubbish
That I have no room to let you in
My dream
Is to be with my vision.
Trusting it so much
That I can free these secrets
And carry on
With these strings
That monitor my movement
And keep me dancing in this place
Flying freely
In this winter wind

. . . .

SATURDAY, MARCH 8

The Moments of Lucidity

This fog-land I live in now is not conducive to lucid thought. My state of constant sedation means that I spend more time asleep than awake, starting out each day groggy and discombobulated, without a clear sense of time, place or sensation.

I stumble around trying to find my bearings, sometimes just enough to go to the bathroom before crawling back to bed. Other times I do get up and try to operate a normal routine.

When I write, my thoughts are not so clear—everything is mixed up. I watch my family hover around me, waiting for the four-hour mark when the injections start again.

The objective—at all costs—is to avoid the debilitating anxiety attacks that have overtaken me in recent days.

Most jarring, I had a phone call from my family doctor Leah, following a home visit the other night. Due to some previous commitments, she will not be available over the next couple of weeks. The gist of her call was an apology for not being here for me, and what almost sounded like a goodbye—along with some heartfelt comments about the closeness we have forged over all of these years, and the very real prospect in her mind that I may not be here when she returns.

This is not something that I can take lightly. I suppose I am still in the process of absorbing it. I have been here before, facing what seemed like the imminent end, but this does feel different. Somehow it is less nebulous than what has been speculated in the past.

So this journey evolves, my family around me to keep my meds on track day and night. They can't do enough for me, catching me when I am wobbly, lifting me off of furniture when I need help. It is humbling and, yes, even a bit much sometimes for someone so fiercely independent. But all of this is necessary now, and I am beyond grateful that I am not dealing with this alone.

Lessons in Humility

Please note that there is nothing dignified about what follows.

The butterfly ports imbedded in my skin through which my medication is delivered have become increasingly problematic, so after repeated failed attempts to reintroduce them, we have moved on to "plan B." This is an external pump connected by tubing to my leg. It weighs about a pound and is awkward to carry around, but is necessary as it steadily deposits the medication into my bloodstream. The down side is that the new medication makes me even groggier than before—my reactions have become very slow.

Case in point: Early the other morning I had to go to the bathroom, but by the time this message was received by my brain it was almost too late. Hence, like a three-year-old, I had an accident. This is on the list of what to expect in the final stages, but nonetheless it is beyond humiliating. Again, my sister was right there to come to the rescue, to gently do what she needed to do to soothe my tears, fix the bedding and me.

Due to the many unsuccessful efforts to find tissue on my limbs strong enough to withstand the ports, I have developed a number of abscesses that are failing to heal. Antibiotics are unavoidable now, and the prospect of a move to a hospice bed where the meds can be delivered intravenously is drawing closer. I am ready, in many ways. The stairs in our multi-level townhome are becoming more burdensome, and the toll on my family who are caring for me night and day is clearly not sustainable.

There are angels in our midst
I am not worthy of the attention
But they swoop into this existence
Offering me ribbons of escape
I wrap them around my body
The love seeps into my skin
While I can not fly freely among them
They hold me in this gentle rhythm
Feel the peace

. . . .

THURSDAY, MARCH 13

The Greatest Gifts

This feels like a time to focus on where I am—on watching this failing body and assessing what I have learned.

As I said to Kirk tonight, it is over these rocky times as vanity and humility fall away that a certain strength and resilience is uncovered. I am nearing something as close to self-acceptance as I have ever felt. I am like the Grinch, with a heart that grows bigger and bigger, and in turn opens to receiving more love than I have ever hoped or dreamed I could experience.

This journey has changed all of us in so many powerful ways. We are breaking old patterns and finding new levels of acceptance. I see it deepen within Kirk as he adapts to our new reality. He has stepped up in ways I likely made it very difficult to do in the past, with my controlling nature.

So experiencing all of this—the support of my family, my care providers—could not have been a greater gift, and truly has brought me to a place where the fear and trepidation about where this is taking me dissipates more each day.

I feel ready in a way I haven't felt to date—and this is entirely attributable to the exchanges of love and care that I experience every day. Nothing is the same, and I truly wouldn't have it any other way.

. . . .

FRIDAY, MARCH 14

When Intervention is Welcome

I have come to believe there is something uniquely precious about the men and women who gravitate toward the field of palliative medicine. This morning I had a home visit from the amazing Dr. Ryan from the Victoria Hospice program, whom I had never met before, and a palliative care resident. Dr. Ryan spent almost an hour thoroughly but gently questioning me about my medical history and admitting his unfamiliarity with eating-disorder patients—something that is all too common among the health-care professionals I have encountered over the years. I say that not in a judgmental way, but I could see that even talking about this cohort of patients—men and women who, like me, are not teenagers and have dealt with these illnesses for decades—was instructive to both the physician and the resident.

But the most significant aspect of the visit was their assessment of two large and painful abscess areas on my chest from which the plastic butterfly ports had to be removed. The abscesses are growing larger and failing to drain after almost a week.

The prospect of the infection going septic was of sufficient concern that after we said our goodbyes, the doctor immediately made contact with a general surgeon. Before I knew it I was off to the hospital emergency room where the abscesses were promptly surgically drained, packed with an antiseptic material and bandaged up. Overall, and despite the hordes of walking wounded in the waiting room, I was in and out in a record two hours.

I had underestimated the serious prospect that if they were to turn septic in my bloodstream, they could actually shorten my lifespan. Despite my insistence on limited interventions, this is something I couldn't justify. So away I go with another adventure in health-care land, offering my profound thanks to the remarkable physicians who took the time to treat a palliative patient with dignity, respect and a minimum of fuss.

. . . .

SATURDAY, MARCH 15

The Fine Print

Relatively early in my journey, my lovely family doctor and I put together an advance care plan. I remember her reminding me that it is a legally binding document, and that I ought to be careful about how prescriptive I wanted to be about what interventions I did and did not want to prolong my life.

Her prophetic words came back to me with a vengeance yesterday when I realized that something as simple—and as easily treated—as a septic wound or a urine infection could actually end my life.

While I was clear that I wanted a Do Not Resuscitate (DNR) order, it was decided that other treatments should not be ruled out, providing they were easy to take care of and would provide comfort. Since this whole approach is predicated on comfort measures, we agreed that we would deal with those issues as they arose.

Yesterday was one of those watershed moments, and I didn't hesitate to say, "Yes, let's deal with it—and sooner rather than later." It would seem wrong, after all of this, to let something as trivial as an infection lead to my demise. Not that I am bargaining for more time—I am as prepared as I could possibly be for what will come naturally. But nor am I ready to completely capitulate to smaller bumps along the road.

. . . .

SUNDAY, MARCH 16
When The Sun Just Won't Shine

Today has been tough . . . very tough. In fact, it has been a day of some tears, and feeling well and truly sorry for myself.

I think I underestimated the pain and general after-effects of having my infected port sites surgically drained. The process of tending to them every day is very painful, and I generally feel very unwell and wasted since Friday afternoon's procedure.

I have tried so hard to focus on the good—to separate the feelings of my declining body from my emotional state, and to express gratitude as time marches forward. But sometimes I just can't do it. I can't help but feel pain on all levels and it just feels necessary to get it out.

·I want not to be described as brave, because I am just a human being living through an experience over which I have no control— and what has transpired is the result of my own choices and lack of strength. I can't say with confidence tomorrow will be a better day. No day brings certainty, and rising to the occasion is a hope, but not a given.

Need to Know Basis

Another day, and the worst part of it is mercifully over, after a visit from the wonderful palliative care response team to address the daily aftermath from Friday's surgical procedures. My mom was by my side, squeezing my hand during the hardest part when the tears were flowing.

I learned today that there are only four cities in B.C. and Alberta that offer this kind of home-based 24/7 service for palliative patients—and they rely largely on fundraising to keep going. To think this godsend might fail to be maintained for patients like me terrifies me. The prospects of either having to leave the house to see my care team, or be lodged in a hospital bed at huge expense, simply seem illogical and wrong. During these rougher times, I am entirely dependent on the care and counselling that they bring so compassionately each day, as well as their experience and wisdom. Added to that, I can't imagine taking the risk of being exposed to further infection in hospital, were this option not available where I live.

Nurse Jill told me honestly today that she sees a frailer version of me than in her previous visits. The context of our discussion was the fact that I have given up the monthly lab work. In the hospice world this lab work is considered largely unnecessary, as the chances of it legitimately inducing any shift in the treatment plan are slim to none. Instead, the focus has been on finding the right blend of medications to keep me as comfortable as possible as my body goes through its natural shutting down.

But now, several months having passed since the latest lab work was processed and noted, there is still a big part of me that craves those numbers—even if it changes nothing.

It's not just curiosity that compels me to know—it is about affirming what I feel physically and mentally to be true—to find my experience reflected in that long list of numbers. But in other ways, I acknowledge it is a fool's errand. The numbers won't answer the question that continues to hang over my head of just how close I am to the end, and they could easily cause more anxiety than comfort.

That impulse is more about my life force battling with what is occurring naturally. In choosing to address these infections, for example, I made a deliberate intervention into a process that would have inevitably expedited the move toward death. So, this dichotomy is important to acknowledge. No other map exists of where I will go from here.

· · · · · · · · · ·

TUESDAY, MARCH 18
Love Beyond All Measure

I don't believe you can fully appreciate what the people you love are capable of—the resilience of their spirit and their capacity for love—until you find yourself in a situation that tests them the way my family and loved ones have been challenged over the past year. I have watched them grow and change in ways I couldn't have anticipated before my diagnosis and the subsequent deterioration of my body; my growing dependence and increasingly frailty. I marvel at their love for me; at their unending patience and generosity.

As my reserves to fight are all but exhausted, there is a strong chance I may not have what it takes to heal from my recent infections. Thus, my family and I face another new round of emotions—another shift in my medication regime, and a growing realization that the time ahead may not be as open-ended as we have clung to in recent months. We are still absorbing this information and processing as best we can. And yet I woke up this morning with a sense of peace, secure in the knowledge that I am surrounded by all of the love and support I need to take on what is to come. I must repeat that even through the days of pain and waning spirits, in so many respects this year has been the best time in my life—a time of growth, self-awareness and love that I cannot fully put into words.

. . . .

FRIDAY, MARCH 21

When It Is Truly Time To Say It Is Over

For reasons I really don't want to explain, this will be my final blog post.

In many ways having this outlet has saved me this year, giving me a way to express what this path has been like; to reveal honestly how I came to this place, to make amends as best I could and to express my gratitude to everyone who has reached out to me through all of the ups and downs.

If I have been graphic at times—perhaps a little too revealing—it is only because I have spent so many years living in denial. Coming clean about my journey has been so very healing to me in ways I can't fully express. I beg you please not to push me privately or publicly to say how I came to this decision. It is simply time to end this. My thanks again for the gift of your love and support and your indulgence in following along with me.

Things Left Unsaid

I feel like I have left some rather large question marks about why I came to the decision to end my blog the other day.

First, it began with one of my regular visits from the palliative response team late last week. While the overwhelming majority of nurses who have followed these pages have been effusive in their support of the advocacy I have attempted on their behalf, I was informed that some of the comments I had made on this blog over the course of the past few months had made some nurses feel concerned for their safety.

This news shook me in a way I cannot describe. To those nurses who had concerns, I can only say that I am eternally sorry. While it was only ever my intention to draw attention to the amazing work they do, and in particular the unfailing support they have provided to both myself and my family, I am also aware that many of the scenarios they walk into are dangerous and precarious to say the least. Unco-operative patients and unpredictable family dynamics can often make them feel at risk, particularly in the nighttime hours.

Second, my symptoms have worsened to such a degree that my capacity to maintain the energy to lucidly keep up with this communication and even respond to some of my dearest friends has been compromised in such a way that it feels difficult to carry on the way I have been. My ups and downs have become more alarming—so much so that when my family doctor saw me two weeks ago she honestly believed I would not last to see her return.

Third, my quality of life has become narrower and narrower as many of the things I used to enjoy—my love of reading, for example—I simply cannot do anymore as I lack the basic concentration to keep up. My appetite has worsened, leaving me able to ingest only an increasingly narrow list of foods. I barely leave the house anymore, if at all. And overall, I am no closer to knowing how long I will have to endure this than I was before.

As I have told my family and my doctor in all honesty, if there was a pill I could take to end this, I would. But, in this country this is not a legal option for me.

In short, I am tired and ready in all ways for this to come to an end—something that right now is not under my control.

April
2014

Second Thoughts

This blog has only ever been my voice, my thoughts. I never purported to speak on anyone else's behalf or tried to convince anyone that my way of seeing things or handling this would be right for anyone else.

As my life and my contact with the outside world gets smaller and smaller, losing this—my only remaining outlet—has been like losing a limb. Since I was a little girl, the only way I really knew how to get my feelings out was to write them down. Frankly, as long as this keeps dragging on, I need this blog for no one else's sake but my own.

Someone wise once told me that people who have been fighters all their life find the end stages more difficult to accept, while those who have lived a more passive life find it easier to let go. I suppose the people who know me well know which category I fall into. So, perhaps it is not that surprising that I find it as difficult as I have to give in, even though everything in my being is ready for this all to stop.

I have spent a lot of time on the website of the Right to Die Society of Canada, which makes it clear that, in this country, it is the connections you have that determine who really has the option to pursue their choice. To me, it is clear from this that it is happening in a covert way, probably far more frequently than we realize.

Although the website has links to a lot of practical information on how to carry out an assisted death, I have been warned that without the help of a qualified professional, things can and have gone horribly wrong—and the prospect of doing something that would actually prolong this is more than I can bear. So for now I will write when my energy permits me to do so. For me, not for anyone else, because frankly it feels like all I have.

· · · · · · · · · ·

THURSDAY, APRIL 3
Dreams

Despite the fact that I live with the imminent prospect of death, as these days drag on I don't exactly spend every waking moment thinking things are going to just suddenly stop. For one thing, after all the years of punishment, my heart still keeps going, as my nurses have reiterated many times. But lately at night, something in my subconscious is obviously fixated on the prospect of leaving this mortal coil.

I wouldn't exactly call them dreams—more like nightmares that seem to go on and on, so much so that I often dread the night-time as it is approaching. They follow pretty similar themes. I hear people in our house, family and friends from far and near, having conversations together, and I find myself trying and failing to get to them. Or I am calling out to them, but no one can hear me, and I am unable to be part of what is going on. I guess in the night I can visualize what it will be like not to be here—not to be part of the life I once knew.

I have heard so many predictions of when this might end, and none of them have come to fruition. As I am continually told, I am one of less than a handful of patients who have this particular blend of issues, so everything is a guess and speculation. As parts of my body are shutting down and my energy fades more and more each day, I continue to worry about how things will go from here.

I am sure anyone in my position would understand these questions—how the waiting can be excruciating in ways I can't convey, not just for me, but for the people who love me. So, after many weeks of Kirk's being away from work, we have decided it is better that he go back for now, as there is nothing more we can do but wait. And the reality is, his presence here—or that of my family—will not prevent whatever is to come. More than that, it is long overdue that he should have some respite from this space. It is the right thing to do. His co-workers have been miraculously understanding and generous for the time he has already taken.

So things will change again—something that has been constant in this process. We are as ready as we can be for things to go back to what they were, for however long this lasts. I still have the support of my family and care providers, so it is not like I am completely alone.

. . . .

FRIDAY, APRIL 4

How Are You?

"How are you?" This is an unavoidable question for someone in a circumstance like mine, but in all honesty, not one that I feel enthusiastic about responding to.

Things change, but not necessarily in a good way. I don't even know how to answer some days. It seems petty of me to not respect that people are asking out of love or genuine concern, but as I am more and more distant from people who were once a constant presence in my life, it feels weird to express whatever I am feeling at any given moment.

I feel more and more like a guinea pig for changing drug regimes that start out promising, then leave me back where I started, or worse.

I guess I am tired; frustrated by my lack of independence that was always such a huge part of my life. The word "dependence" is the worst possible word that I can think of right now. I push and push not to ask for help, and feel so guilty when I have no alternative but to do so.

I don't expect people to stop asking. I'm just saying that sometimes it is hard to say where I really am, what I really need or want, when I can't even figure it out myself.

. . . .

Another vacant weekend passes
I sit at the window
And life drives by
I can see it clearly
But I can only watch that highway
I've become intractable
World is becoming smaller
I've curled up and feel
the edges with my palms

. . . .

SATURDAY, APRIL 5
Purgatory

I grew up in the Catholic faith because, like most kids, I did what my parents did, without questioning or really understanding what the church stands for. Along with the takeaways of fear and incredible guilt, one thing I did learn from it is the concept of purgatory—that alleged limbo between heaven and hell. If I had to describe in a word where I am right now, purgatory seems as appropriate as anything. I am living a quarter of the life I lived before, primarily housebound, and with very little that I feel capable of changing.

Even my doctor remains perplexed by my body failing, then bouncing back to a state where my organs somehow hang on. Nothing terrifies me more than going on like this indefinitely.

There is something almost akin to the boy who cried wolf. The word of my impending death is deeply felt by many who care for me, and so it is almost like an embarrassment that things change so slowly. But as hard as this is to say, nothing gives me less comfort than when people interject their own religious beliefs in their effort to be consoling. Beliefs are deeply personal, and the assumption that I share them could not be further from the truth. I do have my own belief system that I have come to after many years, and which is entirely personal. While I respect other people's faith, I don't believe it is anyone's right to assume it is welcome or comforting to impose those beliefs on me, no matter how well-meaning they may be.

I feel guilty for raising this, but I would urge people to think long and hard before sharing with me or any other palliative patient their own thoughts on the "afterlife." I am not looking for conversion at this stage of my journey. Beliefs are not facts. They are just concepts that some people seem to find comforting—which is fine and even admirable. But please never assume that I, or anyone else, necessarily share that point of view.

The Here and Now

Someone very wise reminded me yesterday of the importance of focusing on the here and now—never a strong suit of mine. My tendency has been to project into the future scenarios over which I have no control, or pick at things from my past that can never be taken away.

For some weeks now I have been feeling that there isn't a lot about where I am that I am anxious to embrace, or even accept. I am simply not there right now.

I also know that there really is no alternative but to find some kind of acceptance for where I am—fighting it has clearly been less than effective.

I'm not exactly feeling enlightened about how I might accomplish that. I do try to focus on the things I am grateful for—considering the many ways in which people suffer that I cannot even imagine. For now, all I can do is to try—a tall order, but one that I am trying hard to accept.

· · · · · · · · · ·

WEDNESDAY, APRIL 9

What is Not So Easy to Block Out

A month ago yesterday was one of my darkest days since this whole odyssey began. But only recently, I learned some unsettling things about that day—things of which I have no recollection.

I was a total mess on that day—so unsettled that I spent over 12 hours wandering through the house, unable to sit, lie down, or find any place that was comfortable. Eventually, my sister had to hold on to me as I grew weaker, all while still wandering endless circles around our living room. Eventually a nurse came to the house and even my family doctor paid a visit at 6 p.m.

What I didn't know is that at one point she pulled my sister aside and suggested she contact my family in case there was anything they wanted to say to me before I was eventually sedated. I still don't remember it, but everyone in my family came that night. My mom and dad drove in from Duncan, my nephews and my sister and brother-in-law David... and I actually spoke to them before I was finally settled for the night. Again, these are moments I don't remember.

It is hard for me to think of these events and realize how close to the end things seemed at the time—and yet still I am here, somehow going through these experiences and unfortunately taking my family with me.

Perhaps that is why now I find myself pushing them away to some degree, discouraging visits, managing phone calls. Initially, I thought that I wanted desperately not to be alone near the end. Maybe I am in a different space now.

Things have turned again since that time. I haven't had a significant repeat of that day, but it sticks with me, haunting me—the fact that these things could have happened and yet I blocked them out so completely from my mind.

It is all so unpredictable, where I will be at any given moment. That is why the whole notion of focusing on the here and now seems the only way to live through this. I simply don't know how long I can or will continue to live this way, so each day I wait—for something that seems impossible to envision.

Adventures in the Outside World

Yesterday was the first day I left the house in about a month. The occasion was that my sister was taking me to get my hair cut.

Leaving the house is an impossible ordeal, which is remarkable, considering my life before. The thing I can't get used to is the weakness that goes along with it—being helped in and out of my sister's car like an invalid.

But the worst moment was when we finally made it into the salon. I tried to get out of the chair to get to the sink and stumbled, narrowly missing knocking everything off my stylist's station, correcting myself just before I fell to the floor. It may sound like a minor incident, but it felt entirely humiliating at the time.

It is this that I find hardest to accept—the simple things I once took for granted, slowly becoming harder to accomplish. Feeling like my memory and my thoughts are becoming so jumbled that I can't express what I want or need to say at any given time.

This was not the only humiliating moment of my day, but I will spare you the details. Suffice it to say that this is all part of the territory. And no matter how resilient I have been, these things are part of this ride that I have no other option but to accept, no matter how much I want to block them out.

My family is sympathetic. They feel bad on my behalf. But no amount of their efforts to soothe me can take it away entirely. So, today the sun is shining, and I am staying put, trying my best to put it behind me, one day at a time and all that. No place to be except where I am.

The Valiant Battle of Gloria Taylor

Last night, with some trepidation, I watched a documentary profiling Gloria Taylor—the brave B.C. woman with ALS who took her battle for the right to a dignified death assisted by a physician to the courts.

Sadly, she passed away before the case ultimately made it to the Supreme Court—in a hospital, not in her home as she had hoped.

It was painful to watch, not only for the indignities she suffered, but for the interviews with her family members who painfully watched her waste away and so eloquently shared many of their last moments with her. Being forced to ask for help to get off the toilet in a hotel bathroom when a friend was unable to assist her; gradually unable to receive the relief from a pain clinic as her muscle mass wasted away . . . It felt all too close to home, and yet I couldn't look away.

She lived a year longer than the doctors had predicted, and it just reminded me of how excruciating it is not to know how much longer this will go on.

More transitions are happening to me—the itchiness that is a byproduct of the renal disease has returned in the last week with a vengeance. I sleep more and more each day, sometimes up to seven hours in total through the morning and afternoon. I feel weaker, and yet I fight every day to do the simplest things without help—showering, making a cup of tea.

I know I won't be able to keep this up forever, and will eventually need constant babysitting from my family members, but knowing when to ask for that help is so hard for me to figure out, and my seemingly insatiable desire to get through this myself becomes more and more unrealistic.

As confident as I am that I have made all of the necessary preparations for the end, not knowing what to expect next seems the most bitter pill to swallow. And I find fear setting in, in a way it hasn't before, about the ultimate transition that I know is coming.

I wish I had the belief that so many people cling to about what happens when that moment comes, but I simply don't have a clue about what to expect.

I seem to lack the capacity to take comfort in what many people envision about the end of life. That is just not where I am, and I don't see that changing. And yet, a part of me prays for a painless end—going quietly in my sleep with a minimum of fuss or helplessness—anything to spare my loved ones more pain than they have already experienced.

I should be grateful for these days, and yet I feel nothing but resentment now. Knowing that the court's efforts continue to drag on, it just seems so patently unfair that we can't make decisions for ourselves. Without professional help, the options that exist are risky and, for the most part, unrealistic.

I desperately hope that the courts will do the right thing and recognize the suffering that is going on daily for thousands of Canadians who are the object of valiant efforts by the health-care system to keep them going, regardless of how miserable their quality of life. Serenity just doesn't seem like too much to ask for, does it?

. . . .

Michelle entered hospice care at Saanich Peninsula Hospital on Monday, April 21—Easter Monday. She did not write again.

She had spent the previous Easter weekend (2013) in hospital as well—it was the weekend she received her diagnosis.

Epilogue

This is the Sound Of One Voice—The Final Verse

Those of you who have been reading this blog for the past several months will know that the wonderful and talented woman who composed it—my sister, Michelle—was in the end stage of renal failure after living most of her life with a dual eating disorder. You will also know that Michelle, always 'Chelle to her family, eventually stopped posting for a few different reasons, primarily because she no longer possessed the energy to write. But she had one post, composed five months ago, which she had reserved as her last, and which she asked me to publish for her when her journey finally ended.

Michelle—my beautiful, intelligent, funny, generous, loving "little" sister—died yesterday. Her passing was peaceful. She simply took a last breath, and then did not take another. Her last few days were calm, happy. She told Kirk, her beloved partner, that she was "happy every day" and that she had "so much to be grateful for"—the view outside her window, the loving people she had around her, her two "wee white pups" (Samuel and Daisy), the beautiful messages from family, friends and colleagues who sent so much love to her . . . She repeated those same sentiments to our mom and to me; she felt loved and cared for, and all was good in her world.

We are grateful that her final days were so free of the pain she carried with her through most of her life. She was an extraordinary person, with many, many gifts that, most of the time, she could not see in herself. But we saw them, and we are richer for having had her in our lives.

So, this is the sound of one voice, my sister, Michelle, sharing her last words with the world. I miss you so very much already, my wee one. I'll love you forever, my darling girl.

xo

—*Karen Flello*

. . . .

I don't know when or if this will be read, but I know someone else's hand will post this—hit the button that says "publish" and let it go. It will mean that this part of the journey—my journey—has come to an end.

The powerful indigenous writer Thomas King wrote: "The truth about stories is, that's all we are." This blog—my stories, my presence here—mattered to me in a way that is hard to express. I wanted more than anything to tell the truth—an experiment with no particular agenda or deeper meaning. And yet what I discovered was that it was possible to share the parts of yourself you have hidden from the world—even from yourself—and that transformative things could happen. People began to open up to me in a way I never dreamed possible. Far from letting me go, they just held on tighter.

I learned you could walk away from everything that defined you and discover something deeper, when the trappings of the working world are gone. That the downward journey—letting go of many of the things one surrounds oneself with to fill the empty spaces—brought its own freedom. That the moments that matter are the connection of people's stories and souls and other broken pieces that I have stumbled across, all bringing their own healing power.

It was worth the pain.

—*Michelle Stewart*

Acknowledgments

To my mom and dad, my sister, Karen (David, my sweet Liam, my angel Andrew),

How can I possibly express to you what you mean to me—how much I will miss wrapping my arms around you? Know I will always be with you. Always with love. To my baby brother Murray—my precious angel—I love you, our forever wee boy. To Aaron, Shannon, Aanji and Binaawke, for every joyful moment and the gift of you, my gratitude and endless love. For the privilege of being called "Nana," which filled me with delight. To Miranda, Nathan and the new little soul joining your family, my thanks for the love, the light, the happiness you brought me. And to the baby I may never hold, you have shone brightly in my heart. May your life be a gift of abundance and joy. To those relatives, friends, colleagues and acquaintances who lightened my path and enriched me with your presence, may you be surrounded always with peace and love.

And, finally, to Kirk. Tirkie. There are no words to describe how I feel about what I might have missed had fate not brought us here. The gifts of your family, your kindness, your incredible heart. More than anything, I wish you a full life, free of pain, surrounded by everyone who loves you (and they are legion). In the beautiful words of Christine McVie: "For you, there'll be no more crying... for you, the sun will be shining..."

In the end, this has been the sound of one voice—one voice that may echo in your mind, telling you I love you...I love you...I love you...